The Fool's Journey through the Tarot

~ Cups ~

Noel Eastwood

Book 4 The Fool's Journey Series

All rights reserved, copyright © 2021 Noel Eastwood

Noel Eastwood asserts the moral right to be identified as the author of this work. By payment of the required fees, you have been granted the non-exclusive and non-transferable right to access and read the text of this ebook on screen or in print form. No part of the text may be reproduced, transmitted, downloaded, decompiled, reverse engineered, stored in or introduced into any information storage or retrieval system, in any form or by any means, electronic or mechanical, known or otherwise yet invented, without the express permission of Noel Eastwood.

This novel is a work of fiction set in the context of Tarot and other esoteric wisdom. Characterisation, incidents and locations portrayed are the work of the author's imagination. It is stressed that the contents of this book are in no way a substitute for personal supervision by a qualified medical or psychological professional. It is recommended that you consult your health professional if you wish to compliment your treatment with meditation, self-hypnosis or any of the techniques described herein. If you have an underlying psychological condition or are in crisis, please seek professional help. The author and editors accept no responsibility for outcomes if you use the techniques described in this book. No affiliation is implied or intended with any organisation or recognisable body mentioned within.

To contact the author, Noel Eastwood:
Email: info@plutoscave.com
Web: http://www.plutoscave.com
Facebook: @PlutosCave
Editor: Kristal and JoAnn
Cover: Peta Fenton
Tarot deck: Original Rider-Waite deck (1910)

Table of Contents

Authors Foreword

Ace of Cups

Two of Cups

Three of Cups

Four of Cups

Five of Cups

Six of Cups

Seven of Cups

Eight of Cups

Nine of Cups

Ten of Cups

Ten of Cups

Astrological Correspondences with the Tarot

Keywords – Cups Meanings

Taoist Water Meditation

About the Author

Author's Foreword

I have enjoyed the challenge of portraying the Tarot minor arcana suits in a story format that is both entertaining and enlightening. In aligning the story with each card and esoteric theme of the suits, readers have found that it brings the lessons of the Tarot cards to life. To achieve this I have continued to use the technique of scrying: meditating on the imagery and symbols within each card. This has enabled me to describe the card's meaning in Follin's meditations at the end of each chapter.

The Cups suit represents the esoteric element of Water, as such, it rules emotions, particularly those involved with compassion, courtship and personal relationships. However, Aphrodite, and her son, Eros, will often leave the door ajar allowing entry of other, less pleasurable Cups emotions. This can sometimes present as disturbing thoughts and feelings that frequently plague human relationships. I have endeavoured to demonstrate how this plays out in real life using the Cups cards as my guide.

I'd like to remind you once again that the interpretations are mine, not everyone will agree and that is fine. The magic of Tarot is in the variance of interpretations for each of its symbols. For every Tarotist, there is a unique interpretation based on their personal life experiences and pathway to Tarot. I don't want you to think that your meditations or interpretations need to be identical to mine, that would be to entice folly. As always, seek your own insights and be true to your mystics quest, the Fool's Journey.

Regards and best wishes on your path of discovery
Noel Eastwood - Australia, 2021
Psychotherapist, Astrologer, Tarotist

"The best and most beautiful things in the world cannot be seen or even touched. They must be felt with the heart." **Helen Keller.**

Chapter 1 - Ace of Cups
Initiating intimacy and nurturing.

Follin, Eve and their Swords escort arrived mid-morning at their rendezvous, the Cups fishing village of Weathersea comfortably situated at the mouth of the River of Cups. There were baskets of fresh seafood laid out in the market square displaying a variety of shellfish; oysters; crabs and lobsters in huge pots; and there were still plenty of fresh fish being carried off the fishing vessels.

Follin greedily breathed in the mosaic scents of the salty sea air and the produce from the sea itself. It reminded him of his childhood, of the times his father took him to the local fish markets near their village. Large fishing boats bustled with activity as the sailors carried the last of their catch to the market stalls. As Follin and Eve walked along the wharf they listened in delight as the sailors sang lustily while they worked, keen to finish up and retire to their homes after a busy night fishing the estuaries and open seas.

Everyone in the market was busy, excitedly talking as they bought and sold the local produce be it hot tea and coffee; warmed honey-mead; fresh-baked bread rolls; fresh vegetables, and of course every variety of seafood imaginable. To the two Mystic Islanders, it was a wonderful break from the dry, dusty Swords plains and the dense forests of their journey from the Swords castle. They revelled in the playful bustle and merriment evident in the banter among the fishermen, stallholders and market-goers.

"This is a madhouse!" exclaimed the Swords Page Arthur, a broad smile on his face as he joined in the spirit of the markets. "Everyone seems to be infected with friendliness. They must be smoking some of that magic fungus Ziggy told us about."

The others laughed with him as they too took in the euphoric atmosphere of Weathersea's fish markets. Even the normally quiet Sir William smiled when one of the stallholders offered the Swords Knight a plate of fresh oysters. The fishmonger laughed loudly as the newcomers huddled close to feast from his tray. His leather apron and straw hat appeared to be part of each stallholder's uniform. To Follin's delight, the stallholders appeared to be clones of each other in their dress, banter and mannerisms.

"Choice oysters for your plate, sirs and misses. When you've finished this lot come on over to the Blue Marlin stall. That's the one with the big blue marlin flag - of course," he chuckled. "I'll have my boy open you another dozen… or ten, but," he whispered conspiratorially, "a little currency would be appreciated in return." The fishmonger laughed again as Page Natalie grabbed Arthur by the hand and dragged him towards the Blue Marlin stall.

From out of the crowd strode a royally-dressed couple, Pages of the Cups Kingdom. In their hands, they carried garlands of flowers to welcome the two Mystic Islanders. They invited their guests to make their way to an enormous tent filled with wooden tables heavily loaded with food and drink.

"Welcome to Weathersea, one of the busiest fishing ports in the Cups Kingdom. I'm Page Jon and this is my wife, Page Kahmia. We're here to escort you to our capital, the City of Life."

The youthful Pages bowed deeply to Follin and Eve. "Sir Rohan sends his apologies, he's currently busy arranging our passage in the Storm Chaser. He will be with us shortly."

"I have a set of drawings for you too, Follin," announced Page Kahmia politely. "The King asked me to deliver them to you." She handed Follin a sheaf of folded papers which he put inside his jacket to examine later. These were symbolic illustrations of his lessons through the Cups Kingdom. Follin couldn't wait to study them.

Page Kahmia turned to Sir William, the Knight of Swords, who had just finished speaking to his commander of cavalry regarding their troop's meals and sleeping arrangements. "Sir William, we are honoured to see you once again. It would please us to have your escort join us at our meal tent. We have refreshments and the village common has been cleared for your men to set up their tents." Page Kahmia curtsied then turned to speak to Sir Darwyn and Ziggy, she spoke in the Elven tongue.

When she finished she turned to Follin and Eve. "I have invited our cousin, Ziggy, to join us. He is always a welcome visitor to our community, as is Sir Darwyn, our chivalrous Charioteer." It was obvious to Eve and Follin that these were all close friends.

As the group were chatting the Swords wagon train pulled into the village common and the soldiers began to set up their accommodation. Some of the Swords soldiers came from this region and were familiar with the Weathersea village markets. They were keen to get their share of fresh seafood before it was sold out.

The Cups Knight, Sir Rohan, was making the final arrangements for their transport with the captain of the Storm Chaser, Captain Luddson. When Sir Rohan had finished, he spied the newcomers and strode purposefully through the busy markets towards them. He opened his arms wide as he approached Ziggy, Sir Darwyn and the Swords Knight, Sir William, grabbing each in a firm embrace.

"Well this is a wonderful surprise!" he roared. "What a pleasure to see you cousin Ziggy, and you William. And I see that reckless warrior, Sir Darwyn, is here as well. What a wonderful time we're going to have." His face beamed as he led the group towards the meal tent.

Follin and Eve didn't want to leave the markets. It felt as if they were caught up in an alternate universe. The stall-holder conversations were hypnotic, they chatted away cheerily as they bustled the couple off to their various stalls. There they handed them gifts of fish, lobsters and anything else the two could fit in their arms. Page Kahmia had to rescue their visitors before they collapsed under the weight of the Cups generosity.

"Oi! Page Kahmia! Give these two a hand will ya, love? I hear they're from the Mystic Isle and that sort of makes 'em relatives, don't it?" yelled one old woman holding tightly to Eve's arm guiding her through the throng of well-wishers.

Page Kahmia thought for a moment. "Hmm, maybe you're right, Grandmother, they could be related to us... I'll ask the Queen, she knows those sorts of things."

The two Swords Pages, Arthur and Natalie, had accompanied Follin and Eve, their arms too were also weighed down with parcels of fresh seafood.

"I think they might have Cups ancestry, Kahmia. Look at their hair, it's the same yellow that you, Jon and many of the Cups have," cried Natalie above the noise and bustle of the market. "I've been working on their heritage all year. I suspect they have some elven blood too, as you do. It's a pity I can't go with you when you speak with the Queen, she's my favourite aunt." Natalie tugged at Arthur's arm as Kahmia steered them towards the main tent behind Sir Rohan.

It was a day of wonder for Follin and Eve, everyone was so kind and generous. By the time they had 'second lunch', Follin had to go outside for a break. He needed to walk off his many servings of oysters and lobster. Page Jon jumped up when he noticed that the very member of the troop he was commanded to safeguard, was leaving. Winding his way through the mass of gaily chattering soldiers, cooks and their helpers, Jon raced to catch up with Follin.

"Phew! Follin, slow down a bit, please. Can I show you around the village?" he panted as he caught up with his ward.

"Hi, Jon. I was just going for a walk to settle my stomach. I've never seen so much seafood - and never have I seen so much devoured by so few, so quickly, as I have today." Follin grinned to himself, he was quite right too. Where he came from food was a resource accrued with difficulty and even more carefully dispersed. "In my village, we sometimes had fights over who had the rights to the eels when they made their migrations into the streams. My father always kept out of the arguments because he was a mage and mages never take sides in matters of the village. But not my mother, she had three hungry children to feed, plus all the sick villagers who visited my father for healing. During the war, food was more precious than freedom."

Jon gaped, then he caught himself. "Follin, I, I never knew something as common as eels would be worth fighting over. My Kingdom has food for the taking, you just need to make a small effort, that's all." After a moment of reflection, he continued. "I'm sorry to hear that other Kingdoms suffer from starvation. We've always had plenty of food, since, well, since..." he put his fingers to his chin, thinking. "No, I can't recall anyone ever say that they had to fight for a meal in our Kingdom, ever."

"When the Wildlanders invaded our isle I was still in school. It was before I left on my first journey through the Tarot Empire. The Wildlanders ransacked and burned villages, they also brought disease which spread like wildfire. My big brother died of the plague and it broke my father's heart. That was a bad time..."

Follin's voice faded into silence, finally he stopped walking to sit on the wharf overlooking the water, remembering. He dangled his legs over its wooden beams and swung his feet back and forth. Tears formed at the corners of his eyes and he wiped them away with the back of his hand. There was something in the bustle of Weathersea and the scent of the sea that made him melancholic.

"I'm sorry for you and your family, Follin. We've had plague too. The long-haul ships sometimes bring it with them. But we've never been invaded and we've never had starvation, not like you've experienced." Jon put his arm around Follin's shoulder and said softly, his own voice choked with emotion, "You know what, Follin? I think you've come to the right place. Kahmia and I will look after you, I promise."

Follin wiped his sleeve across his eyes and smiled wanly, he liked this young man.

"Jon, what's that ship? The one with sails like triangles? It's big and fast, look at it cut through the water." Follin's mood had shifted, he had allowed himself to indulge in his grief but then he directed it to move on - he was back in control.

"That's one of those long-haul ships I just mentioned. it goes way over the horizon. They sometimes sail for months to other countries far beyond our Tarot Empire." Jon's voice became excited. "Everyone races to the wharf when they pull in to port. They like to show off their bounty from far-away places. My goodness, the stories they tell. We all think they must make some of them up, they're so impossible. Just think, animals bigger than a house? The sailors say there are entire kingdoms of dragons beyond the seas too - how frightening would that be?"

"Jon, the Tarot Empire has a dragon doesn't it?"

"I've not seen him personally but yes, the Wands are said to have a dragon. Apparently, there were hundreds of them in the Empire. I think that might be why we were able to settle here, no-one else wanted to live so close to them. When our ancestors settled here the dragons controlled the forests and plains around the Mountain of Smoke and Fire. It is said that a mighty Wands mage befriended them and asked permission for his Kingdom to settle in the dragon's territory. That's how the Wands learned about Fire magic," explained Jon.

"What happened to all the dragons if there's only one left?" continued Follin.

"They say the dragons are dying out, a disease or magic, no one really knows. There was one family left in the Mountain of Smoke and Fire until recently. Over the past few years, they've all left except for that single dragon." Jon looked at Follin and shrugged.

By the time they had done the rounds of the marketplace, met the other stallholders and the sailors packing their gear up ready for the evening's fishing, Follin's stomach had settled.

"We were wondering what had happened to you two," said Kahmia as they walked into the meals tent. Natalie stood beside her while Arthur remained seated. The Swords Page appeared to have eaten too much. His face changed colour every few seconds. Completely unconcerned Sox was sitting attentively at the table waiting for another mouthful of flavoursome seafood to be passed to him.

"Arthur's eaten too much shellfish," exclaimed Natalie. "He's allergic to anything with a shell. He always gets sick when we visit Weathersea, especially when he eats scallops. I love them but poor Arthur, he'll be visiting the out-house all night now. Why he insists on stuffing himself with scallops I just don't know."

Arthur forced a weak smile. "Those seared garlic scallops are my absolute favourites, but they don't seem to agree with my delicate Swords stomach. The temptation is great but my will is weak..."

That evening the two Kingdoms celebrated their reunion by partying long into the night.

Although Sir Rohan was middle-aged and much older than his royal cousins across the River of Cups, he was highly respected and much loved. He joined in the horse-play with a passion unmatched by his younger comrades. The Cups Knight sang with gusto as he led the soldiers in songs of battle and deeds of heroism.

"We might not get together very often in these troubled times but when we do it's certainly well worth the wait," laughed Sir William as his cousin, Rohan, carried two Cups sailors on his back into battle with their Swords comrades. Each team, Swords versus Cups, consisted of 'horses' and 'knights' complete with light wooden swords and wicker shields. Their battle cries and laughter could be heard all through the village.

Some of the more sober Swords had brought their ever-present Battles games and were already competing with the best of the Cups gamers. They set up their tables well away from the madness of their wrestling and drinking mates. In another corner of the meal tent were the musicians with their own crowd of dancing and singing revellers.

To Follin and Eve, it was bedlam and the lunatics were in charge of the madhouse. In contrast to their adventures in the

Pentacles Kingdom, no-one seemed to take much notice of rules or orderly behaviour. No one seemed to be bothered either when the tables were knocked over in the middle of their horse-play and celebrations.

The only casualty, besides the sore heads the next morning from too much drink, was Arthur. The young Swords Page missed most of the fun.

The Hindamar Highland's archer, Londar, was also missing for most of the evening. When he discovered that his friend, Arthur, was ill, he refused to leave his side, tending him throughout the night.

Young Londar was a Wildlander archer captured fleeing battle on the Swords plains. He was now a renowned Battles game strategist and everyone wanted him on their team. The Swords soldiers were always trying to poach him for their own Battles clan. His Bowmen friends went to great pains to make up for the loss of his father and uncles on the day he was captured. Arthur, too, was one of Londar's Battles clan team-mates, but his night of shellfish indulgence was the only night Londar and Arthur's team lost to the Swords spearmen clan.

The Cups teams were clearly no match for the competitive and experienced Swords but they did excel at eating and drinking. It was argued that a single Cups sailor could out-drink a dozen hardened Swords revellers. The condition of the Swords soldiers the following morning was proof that the Cups bravado was not just idle boasting.

~

Sox and Molly had the time of their lives as well. For most of the trip, they had played in the inner worlds only venturing out of an evening when the group had made camp and were preparing dinner. While Eve was fine with her elemental disappearing for long periods of time, Follin didn't know what to do about Sox. The fae pup had developed a stubborn mind of his own, when Follin wanted his company he had to go into the inner worlds to find him.

"Arthur, what should I do? I can't just stop what I'm doing to go and find Sox all the time," he complained to his friends. Arthur and Londar nodded understandingly.

"Maybe Ziggy can help. What do you think, Follin?" suggested Arthur.

Follin looked at his friend and nodded. "Yeah, great idea, let's ask him."

They found Ziggy sitting with Sir Darwyn. They were chatting with one of the Storm Chaser crewmen.

Follin waited patiently with his two friends until they had finished their conversation.

"Ziggy, I keep losing Sox," he announced to his friend.

"You what?" asked Sir Darwyn.

"I know what Follin means, Darwyn, it's his dog, Sox. He spends more time running around the inner planes with Molly than with his master." Ziggy turned to Follin. "Elf-wise, what would you like us to do?"

"Well, I can't just go into trance every time I need him, especially when we're on patrol," Follin cried in frustration. "Then when I do find him, he runs away to play some more. He's found a group of Molly's elemental friends and they hide him from me. I just don't know what to do about it."

Ziggy smiled and turned to Sir Darwyn again. "Seems the lad has a problem. What do you suggest my warrior friend?"

Sir Darwyn thought for a moment. "Follin, that dog of yours has become a real pest. The elves on the Swords River have even banned him from their sacred worlds."

Follin's face flushed bright red. "Oh dear, I didn't know that," he said softly.

"Having a fae dog carries a lot of responsibility, Follin," said Ziggy nodding his head in thought. "I think it best that I bind him to you as soon as possible."

The Charioteer added, "Fae pets don't have rules like we do, they have their own rules."

"But aren't you leaving this morning with the rest of the Swords?" asked Follin. Londar and Arthur bent forward to listen to their friend's answer.

"We've been invited to stay a little longer with the kindly Cups people," said Sir Darwyn disarmingly.

Follin's smile spread across his face, but the disappointment was clear on Arthur and Londar's. The long trek back to the Swords castle wouldn't be half as pleasant without their two friends.

~

The soldiers of the two Kingdoms enjoyed each other's company over the past few days, it seemed like one long party to Follin and Eve. Sir William was impatient to resume his cavalry patrols once they had distributed their Weathersea produce. Each wagon was loaded to capacity with salted and smoked seafood. These would be dropped off to the many farms and villages on their return journey to the Swords castle.

"Captain Sheckle!" called Sir William. "Have the squadron form up, we'll send them out to screen our wagons."

"Right you are, sir," the dark-haired cavalry captain replied, eager to get moving after their pleasant rest and recreation.

"Sergeant Poppinjoy!" called the captain. "Inform the troops, we leave within the hour."

There was a flurry of movement and shouted orders as squadron and platoon leaders, wagoneers, cooks and camp helpers, raced to attend to their last-minute preparations. They all knew that it would be a long and weary trip back to the Swords castle.

The Pages hugged each of them promising to stay in touch. Londar shyly accepted the hugs too but wasn't sure what to do with his hands when the girls hugged him closer than his mother ever had.

"Londar, for crying out loud," complained Kahmia. "Here, this is how you hug." She grabbed his hands and placed them around her waist then waited for him. "Well? This is when you are supposed to squeeze, like this."

Follin and Arthur broke into broad smiles watching Londar trying to hide his discomfort. He was obviously relieved when the lesson was over. Hugging a Cups girl, especially one with as many attractive curves as Kahmia, was almost too much for the conservative highlander.

As the Swords troops dipped out of sight towards the Swords River, Follin and Eve's Cups escort boarded their ship, the Storm Chaser. The square-rigged trader would transport them along the scenic south coast to the Cups Kingdom's capital city, the City of Life.

~

Follin's Meditation - Ace of Cups

Follin pulled out the Cups pictures handed to him by Page Kahmia. He always found that the first picture was the most interesting. The Ace image showed a hand reaching out from within a cloud to clutch an ornate cup. The cup overflowed with water as a dove, clutching a cross in its beak, dived head-first into the cup. Droplets of water fell into the water below which was populated by flowering lilies.

'That's a mixture of water and matter, perhaps it shows compassion and service. It must signify that our journey through the Cups Kingdom involves lessons on manifesting compassion and selfless service to others. I hope the other cards show me how to actually do that,' Follin mused.

He brought his mind to the dove and spoke to it. "Little bird, do you have any advice for me regarding my journey through the Cups Kingdom?"

The dove sat on the edge of the Cup and cocked its head to one side, studying him. "I do have something for you: always remember that water can drown those who don't take its virtues seriously."

Follin considered the dove's advice for a moment then said, "I know that water is 'feelings', but how does someone drown in feelings?"

"Cups emotions flow deeply, don't be fooled by their presentation of outer calm. Just as a flood can destroy entire townships, emotions can overwhelm and drown the novice who tries to swim in its turbulent waters," *replied the dove.*

Follin considered the dove's answer. "Does that mean I need to learn how to swim with my own feelings?"

"Exactly. You may prefer to contemplate a slightly different turn of phrase that we sometimes use: the novice drowns in the waters the adept swims in."

Follin sought to clarify the dove's cryptic metaphor. "Does this mean that if I don't control my emotions I'll drown in them?"

"Correct." The dove stretched its wings in readiness for flight. "You have come a long way, Follin. You have learned discipline and determination in the Pentacles Kingdom; clarity of thought and negotiating skills in the Swords Kingdom; now that you are here in the Cups Kingdom you will learn that complex emotions lie deep within the centre of every being. If you don't learn to swim in the swirling waters of the deep unconscious during your time here, then you will surely drown."

Chapter 2 – Two of Cups

Union, the emotional change point.

The Storm Chaser was fully loaded with passengers and goods to be dropped off at the various ports on their passage to the City of Life. Thus began the next stage of Follin and Eve's adventure in the Tarot Empire. Amid shouted orders by the chief mate and the well-practised drill of the sailors on watch, they headed for open waters.

Now that he was aboard, Follin was amazed to find that no matter how big the ship had looked from the wharf, it really was tiny. He could easily walk from one side of the ship to the other in only a few strides. When he went below decks he found that he had to duck low to enter their cramped cabin. There was a narrow bunk but no desk or wardrobe. A sea-chest at the end of the bunk was all they had for storage.

"Welcome aboard the good ship, Storm Chaser," yelled Captain Luddson when he was introduced to Follin and Eve.

"Captain, will we be able to visit the Mystic Isle on our way to the city?' asked an inquisitive Eve.

"Lass, that be another month of sailing past our destination. Besides, Storm Chaser needs to go into dry-dock once we get to the City of Life." Captain Luddson always bellowed when he spoke. "Her hull is crawling with worms and covered in barnacles and weed. Right now we're only making half the speed we should be getting out of her. If you want to go to the Mystic Isle that badly, I can make inquiries for you."

Eve backed away a little to protect her hearing. "Thank you, Captain, but if the Mystic Isles are so far away maybe we won't have time for a visit." Eve thought for a moment then asked, "Captain Luddson, why do the Cups call their city, the City of Life?"

"That be because the first Cups that settled there thought they were in paradise. It was a safe haven after their time wandering the countryside looking for somewhere to settle. It gave them hope and it gave them the life they sought, so they called it the 'City of Life'," he explained in his booming voice.

That evening Ziggy met Follin on his walk around the deck. "Ah, there you are, Follin. Eve told me I would find you out here."

"I love the smells, the wind and the waves. It reminds me of home," replied Follin watching the sea spray rising from the ship's bow.

"Indeed it is a lovely experience, but it is time for me to bond you to Sox. Would you care to join Darwyn and I in your cabin?"

"Of course, but Sox has hidden under the bunk and won't come out."

"Perhaps he will allow me to entice him to join us."

Sir Darwyn and Eve had found some chairs to sit on while Ziggy and Follin sat quietly on Follin's bunk. Molly, Eve's elemental, was enamoured of Ziggy. Though invisible to the crew, she was snuggled up close to the Wood Elf and wouldn't move.

"Ziggy, why does Molly do that? She's like those barnacles Captain Luddson talks about, she's stuck to you like glue," chuckled Follin.

The Wood Elf laughed. "Molly is a forest creature and has never been to sea. Being so far from solid land terrifies her. I'm a forest elf, she knows me and my folk very well, all the earth-dwelling elementals in our region do. If you look around you'll not find a single terrestrial elemental here besides Molly. All of her elemental friends have abandoned her now that we're on the ocean."

"Without his friends to distract him, Sox has to listen to you," offered Sir Darwyn.

Ziggy called Sox to him. Although the fae pup didn't want to move from his hiding place he couldn't resist the elf's call.

"Sox, don't fret, you're safe," whispered Ziggy as Sox crawled from under the bunk and sat close to him. The young dog rested his head in Ziggy's lap next to Molly. He tried to wag his tail but it was frozen in fear. "See Follin, he's scared. Now pay attention because this is how we train elementals and fae animals back home."

Follin watched as Ziggy leaned forward to place his forehead on Sox's. He wasn't sure what Ziggy did but Sox suddenly closed his eyes as though asleep. There then came a soft whine from Sox's throat. The fae dog opened his eyes and began licking Ziggy's face furiously.

"There, now you do it," offered Ziggy, very aware that through this exercise he was exposing his innermost secrets to Sox and Follin.

Follin frowned, quite unaware of Ziggy's sacrifice and torment. "But I didn't see you do anything but touch heads."

Ziggy and Sir Darwyn looked at each other and smiled.

"Come close to me, I'll show you." Ziggy gently touched his forehead to Follin's. The force of energy was so great that Follin immediately swooned and almost disappeared into another dimension.

"Hey, hold on there, Follin, stay with me."

Follin heard his elf friend's voice but his mind was awhirl. The next moment he was inside Ziggy's memories. What the elf had long kept hidden was now stripped bare for Follin to see and experience.

"I seem to be somewhere inside you, Ziggy. Is this a bit like what the god, Pan, did to me?" whispered a confused and somewhat disturbed Follin trying to avoid being witness to his friend's personal memories.

Ziggy's voice came to him like an echo from a long way away. "This is only a fraction of what Pan did to you." Ziggy paused a moment before continuing. "Not only have I needed to bond to Sox but there is now a special bond between you and me, my elf-wise friend. I only ask that you tread softly within my soul."

Follin felt as though he was drunk. "I think I understand, Ziggy... I can see a beautiful elf woman and two little children..." Follin suddenly stopped speaking when he realised that he had just accessed his elf friend's most intimate of memories.

Sir Darwyn sighed knowingly. "Stay focused, Follin. What Ziggy is doing is very powerful, very few elves are skilled enough to do this. It binds even those who don't like to be bound and can backfire if you aren't careful. Sox needs to bond with you so that you both share the one mind and Ziggy is enabling you to do that, but it comes at a cost to each of you," warned The Charioteer.

Ziggy directed Follin to place his forehead against Sox's. In what appeared to take but a few moments the three had bonded as a single entity. With great care, Ziggy then removed as much of his own psychic trace as he safely could from Sox and Follin's minds. The two were now locked in a bond that could only be broken in death.

Slowly Follin returned to his body. He was lying in the bunk with a pillow under his head. Sox was beside him, his eyes not wavering from his master's face.

"What happened? Did I fall asleep?" Follin asked as he automatically jumped out of bed. He landed unsteadily on his feet just as the Storm Chaser lurched and rolled in the wind-swept seas. If Sir Darwyn hadn't grabbed him by the arm Follin would have fallen.

"It's my fault, Follin," answered Ziggy with an expression of concern on his face. "There was so much of my personal memories tangled within you, that when I tried to remove them I exhausted your reserves. You've been asleep all night and half the day. Eve's been with you and Sox hasn't left your side. I'd say our lesson was a success but you may feel drained for a day or two."

As Ziggy and Sir Darwyn stood to leave, Follin asked, "Ziggy, does this mean that Sox will come when I call him?"

Ziggy smiled as he replied, "Follin, Sox will now come to you *before* you call him."

~

It took a few days into their voyage for Follin and Eve to become accustomed to the constant pitching and rolling of the Storm Chaser. To their merriment, they found that the sailor's had some unusual customs and sayings. They made every effort to go up on deck when they heard the ship's bell ring to watch the crew set the sail or perform some other task. It broke the boredom and helped them find their sea-legs. They soon learned that a rope was a stay, and there were many other funny nautical names like bollard, batten, port and starboard. They even learned new songs and some imaginative curses which flew about as the crew worked at their tasks.

Eve was ever curious to learn more about the Cups Kingdom and their people. She remembered how Page Kahmia had welcomed Ziggy as a cousin and that was something she wanted to get to the bottom of.

"Kahmia, please, come and sit with me and tell me about Ziggy and how come he's your cousin." Eve led Kahmia onto the deck where she found a place out of the chill wind where they could talk. She had two cups of coffee, cakes and their hideaway was just big enough for them to squeeze into.

Kahmia slipped in beside Eve and gratefully accepted her hot coffee, wrapping her hands around the mug to warm her freezing fingers.

"Well, you see, our heritage lies in the Elven Kingdom from way back when we migrated to the Tarot Empire and..." she began but was suddenly cut off by Eve.

"What? Migrated? From where?" interjected Eve. "I'm sure Mage Hermes said you came here from another world. That's why the Wildlander mages are so keen to be rid of you."

Kahmia held the plate with her honeyed oat cake in one hand while trying to keep her coffee from spilling in the other. She giggled and cake crumbs flew from her mouth as she spoke. "Oh, I'm sorry, Eve, but I just love these cakes. Captain Luddson gets the spices from across the oceans and he keeps the best for himself and his crew. That's why we have coffee, you'll rarely see it in the other Kingdoms, it's way too expensive."

Eve didn't want to get Kahmia side-tracked but she had to admit that she had tried this new beverage when she and Follin were on the Mystic Isle.

"Saoirse village has a small seaport not far from the main village. Captain Luddson told me that his ships sometimes visit there to buy and sell goods," said Eve.

"Of course, I'd forgotten that Captain Luddson trades with the Mystic Isles too, he goes everywhere."

Eve gently steered the conversation back to where she wanted it. "I'm sorry, Kahmia, I think I side-tracked you. You were saying something about the elves and the Tarot Empire?"

"Yes, I was... right." Kahmia paused as she held the last of her cake half-way between the wooden plate balanced precariously on her knee, and her mouth. She quickly licked the honey dripping from her fingers. "The problem was that by the time we arrived on this planet there were people already living here, we called them 'Wildlanders'. The Wildlander leaders are their mages, some are good but there are some real nasty types too. Anyway, The Emperor had to offer them something special so they would allow us to stay."

"What did he offer them?" asked Eve concentrating hard so as not to miss a word.

"He gave them access to some of our Tarot magic and some of Pan's elemental magic, and they gave us some of their lands. You see Pan had decided to waken the elementals early as part of the trade. Those elementals had lain dormant since the dawn of time and weren't supposed to waken for another million years or so." Kahmia finished eating, rubbed her hands together to remove the crumbs and then snuggled deeper under the blanket that Eve had wrapped around them to keep warm.

"But what about Ziggy and the elves, where did they come from?" continued Eve, finishing off her own cake and sipping the last of her coffee. Before she could answer, Kahmia was forced to wrestle against the cold, ocean wind to wrap the blanket tighter around her and Eve's shoulders. They giggled like school-girls when one of the sailors stopped to stare at them in wide-eyed wonder as he passed by on an errand.

"Well, you see, Pan decided that he wanted creatures similar to himself so he made elves. But after a while, he wanted different kinds of people, and that's how Wildlanders came to be created. He made sure he didn't give them any magic though, that would have made them too powerful." Kahmia pulled at the blanket as the ever-persistent wind once again threatened to claw its way into their cosy hideaway.

"Cups are different from the rest of the Tarot Empire though. We were attracted to the warm, southern parts of the peninsula, but the Water Elves were already here. They lived in the boglands, rivers and along the coast. Our ancestors became friends with the elves and intermarried. From those times we became a hybrid. The elves call us 'Merrow', their word for 'water-people', part elf and part human.

"We love it here, it has a warm, pleasant climate and with our Water Elf blood, we need to be near water. So now you know why Ziggy is our cousin, he's an elf. He may be a Wood Elf but we're still related." Kahmia stopped talking as Eve snuggled up close to her for warmth.

Eve thought for a moment then asked, "Kahmia, does that mean Cups are part elf?"

Kahmia explained. "We're part elf, part human, and we just love the beaches. We swim, surf, fish, and just paddle about to have fun in the sun. To us Cups, life holds no joy without a beach. Did we tell you that we have a castle under the sea where the King and Queen live? You'll also discover that every home has a pond. We like to lie at the bottom of our pond and meditate, it relaxes us. We're also a bit magical, it's from our elf blood, but that is a two-edged blade. It makes us extremely sensitive and emotional. You'll notice that we stick together for company because we don't cope with being alone."

Eve became more interested as the conversation developed. "I've got another question. I know you like seafood, but you can't eat fish all the time. What about rabbits, cattle, sheep and fowls, vegetables, and things like hops for beer and grapes for wine?"

Kahmia's face caught a beam of sunlight as she lifted her face and giggled. One of the ship's crew turned when he heard her and smiled, delighting in these attractive young passengers and their joyful laughter.

"Cups love gardening and farming," she said. "In some ways, we're a bit like those boring old Pentacles, we love our flowers and our food. We eat to feel good, eating comforts us. And just like the Pentacles, we can grow anything anywhere. Wait 'till you see our gardens, then you'll understand." Kahmia smiled wickedly at the curious look on her friend's face.

Kahmia explained that the Cups Kingdom was known as the 'food bowl' of the Empire. They would dry, smoke, salt, ferment, preserve, distil or refine their produce before they traded it with the other Kingdoms, and beyond their Tarot Empire borders.

Eve saw that Kahmia took great pride in her Cups heritage. "You said that Cups meditate at the bottom of their pond? How is that possible, you can't breathe underwater?"

"We have a special breathing technique that we learn before we're born. We're even born underwater," replied Kahmia. "There's so much for you to learn while you're here. This is going to be a wonderful time for you and your husband."

At that comment Eve's eyes dropped to stare at her hands. In a subdued voice, she admitted to her new friend, "Kahmia, Follin and I never did have a proper wedding celebration. We just said, 'I wed you', three times like they sometimes do on our island. We didn't have anyone from our family to witness for us."

Kahmia's eyes lit up. "What? You didn't have a proper celebration? My goodness, we can't let you leave here without correcting that!" Kahmia's hands flew about so quickly and erratically that she flicked the blanket off them both. With a shriek and a giggle, she grabbed at it before the wind took hold and whipped it overboard. "I know what we should do. We have a special initiation called the Quest of Life, it's what newlyweds undertake in the Cups Kingdom. Then we can have a big celebration. Eve, you've made me the happiest person alive!"

~

Follin joined Ziggy, Sir Darwyn, Sir Rohan and Page Jon at every opportunity. They would gather on the deck each morning for breakfast and, although he said very little, Follin learned much.

"Yes, the elves were very friendly with my ancestors when they arrived on Earth," said Sir Rohan. "That was well before my time but Ziggy here, he still remembers, don't you Ziggy?"

Follin's eyes opened wide, if Ziggy was present at the time of the Tarot Empire's arrival he must be thousands of years old.

"Yes, I was quite young then, but I do remember, Rohan." Ziggy nodded his head then smiled as he continued. "Like good wine, elves are slow to mature."

"Ziggy, how come elves live so long?" Follin noticed that Ziggy's smile suddenly faded.

His friend looked across the wave tops into the distance as he spoke. "Longevity is both blessing and curse. Sometimes I wonder what it would be like to fear death. To live each day as if it be my last, as humans do. Sadly, I will never experience that pleasure."

Sir Darwyn interrupted the conversation. "Elves have learned to hide their activities from people for their own safety. It's as though they are prisoners in their own lands."

"Darwyn is right, Follin. Once we were kings of the land, we lived in peace and harmony with nature. Elves are sensitive creatures, we feel every vibration around us. We were the first-born humans on Earth. There was such a joy in living back then, but it can be more burden than pleasure in these troubled times." Ziggy abruptly stood and left the group. He stood silently watching the ship's bow cutting through the waves.

Follin excused himself and followed his elf friend. The two stood at the timber rails watching the waves together. For several long minutes, the only sounds were the occasional flap of a sail in the wind and the sounds of the ship surging through the water.

"Ziggy, do you mind if I ask a question?" Follin asked gently.

Ziggy looked at his friend, his eyes had a sadness about them. "Certainly, you are elf-wise and anything you wish to ask is mine to answer."

"What can the elves do? Is there somewhere they can escape to? Somewhere you can find peace?" Follin asked as he fidgeted with one of the stays tied to the timber railing.

"When there are few choices one must accept the inevitable," Ziggy replied softly.

Follin silently pondered his friend's answer. In a soft voice he continued, "Ziggy, I have one more question. You've never spoken of your wife, but I saw something when we were taming Sox and I was wondering..." Ziggy's eyes closed for the briefest of moments and Follin became fearful that he had now crossed the delicate line of their friendship.

Once more Ziggy turned to look at the waves below. With obvious effort, the Wood Elf answered politely. "I was married, Sorcha was her name. You would never find anyone as gentle as she. After many years we were blessed with children, just the two… but then they were all taken from me."

Although he wanted to know more he accepted that their conversation had ended. The moment was broken when Sir Darwyn called for Follin and Ziggy to join them at lunch with the captain.

Captain Luddson entertained his guests in his small but stylishly decorated stateroom. On their arrival, Follin could see that Captain Luddson was in good spirits, but all he ever wanted to talk about was sailing and ships.

The group talked long into the afternoon. Only once did Follin have the opportunity to ask a question, and it was to do with their time of arrival at the City of Life.

"Lad, we be there shortly, just give it a few weeks. Relax, enjoy your journey, there's no need to rush. We've the wind in our sails and the seas are calm this time of year. Ye'll find that the further south ye sail the warmer it gets. Aye, ye can even sit in the sun and the wind at the same time without getting too hot or too cold." The captain laughed which brought on a bout of coughing causing him to spill rum over his jacket.

"Damn and blast!" he cried. The cabin boy was soon there to clean the spill and refill the captain's mug. "We'll soon be passing the cliffs and estuaries along the southern shores. We be putting into some of the villages to drop off mail and supplies, and to pick up produce and passengers. This be what we call the 'meal and mail' section of the voyage, we enjoy it the most. It don't matter none if we stay over an extra night or two. The taverns are well stocked with food, grog and pretty girls. There's always a song and a party along the southern coast."

Page Jon explained further. "Follin, this section of the Kingdom is always a pleasure to visit. Kahmia and I lived there for a while when we were doing our Page training." He paused before moving on to a more important topic of conversation. "Gentlemen, there is a rumour that Follin and Eve are going to undertake the Quest of Life. I was thinking that this would be a good time to prepare Follin for his quest." Jon announced.

"What?" exclaimed an alarmed Follin. "What do I need to prepare?"

"Marriage is challenge enough but here in the Cups Kingdom it starts with a quest - the 'Quest of Life'," replied Jon. "The quest is set to teach the couple to unite as one. If the couple cannot breathe in unison then they are not destined to remain united."

Follin noticed Sir Rohan shift uncomfortably in his seat. The Knight always considered his comments carefully before he spoke.

"Follin," said Sir Rohan softly, "one aspect of the Quest of Life is a test of compatibility. Every couple who successfully undertake the quest have stayed married. Of those who refuse to undergo the quest or fail it, not a single couple has lasted more than a year. This is an opportunity to discover what every prospective couple wants to know - will we stay madly in love?"

Follin felt both excited and frightened. "That means if we pass the quest we will stay together, forever?"

"Yes," replied Sir Rohan soberly.

"In that case, I'm ready," Follin grunted without enthusiasm as he reminded himself that he had never passed a single test in all his years at school.

~

Follin's Meditation - Two of Cups

Follin found himself staring at the picture of the winged lion floating above a man and woman who were sharing a mug of wine. He thought to himself, 'A lion is a wild animal, untameable and ferocious. The set of wings, though, that might indicate there is a spirituality that is higher than our animal urges and instincts. That's an interesting combination.'

The lion stretched his wings luxuriously and began to speak. "Young man, come with me and I'll help you understand what I represent. I want you to get it right because this will be the most important lesson of your stay here."

Follin was now feeling worried, 'the most important lesson' had never promised anything but an enormous problem for him.

The lion took Follin to visit his pride. There were four female lionesses and seven cubs. The lion found a comfortable patch of grass whereupon he rolled onto his back, wriggling in sheer pleasure at the sensual nature of having his back scratched by the stiff, sun-baked grass stalks. Soon several of the lionesses walked over to rub their cheeks on his face. Next, the seven cubs raced over to playfully leap onto his enormous belly. Follin felt within his own heart the warmth and joy in this family reunion. He knew that the lion would sacrifice his life for his family.

"Join me, come on, jump into my skin and feel this, it's just great!" called the lion. Follin did as instructed and felt a sense of unity, a oneness with the lion, his family and his grassland home.

When Follin returned to his body he saw the lion staring at the picture of the Two Of Cups. The lion waited for a long moment before looking across at Follin to await his comment.

"Oh, I see what you are looking at now, the wings. What do they mean?" asked Follin.

"That's easy, just ask yourself, 'what do wings do?'" The lion paused. "Better still, why don't you put the wings on and find out."

Follin reached above his head and pulled the wings down. They embedded themselves in his back and immediately lifted him from the ground to glide gently through the air. He felt excited and alive yet also somewhat disconnected from reality. His perspective had changed from the emotional connection of the lion's family, to one of cold, rational analysis.

"I think I know what you wanted me to understand, master lion," said Follin as he glided back to earth and removed the wings. "The wings mean that if I become totally immersed in my feelings of love, passion and affection, I could lose my down-to-earth perspective. My decisions would be based solely on how I felt at the time. They might be irrational, illogical and based on the moment without regard for the future. I would forget to consider the outcomes and consequences of my actions."

"Correct. Although this picture is similar to the Swords lessons you have already encountered, it has many subtle twists that you will need to learn if you wish to understand the Cups lessons," replied the lion now resuming his position above the happy couple.

"This is the 'change point' isn't it," Follin said. He had learned about the change point in his meditations with the Major Arcana, the Pentacles and the Swords Kingdoms. "Let me see if I can get this right: the lovers unite under the wings of cold logic, and the lion's wild passions. To stay together they need to be prepared to put aside their instinctive emotions so that they can make rational decisions to survive the trials of marriage. They seek to balance cold logic in the face of hot emotions."

"You're getting there, just remember that the Cups people are generous and caring, but they are also wildly emotional. They have a tendency to be swayed by their feelings without recourse to critical analysis of the evidence presented and in consideration of the consequences of their actions. Their challenge is to set boundaries in their relationships to help them manage their extreme mood swings."

The lion reminded Follin that he had yet to interview the young couple in the picture so he introduced himself to them.

"Hello, I'm trying to understand the message of your picture. Can you please explain what 'boundaries' are?" he asked.

The young man spoke first. "The first thing you must realise, Follin, is that people form partnerships for love, companionship or even just to satisfy their physical needs. Once formed many people can easily become lost, losing their sense of identity. Some may fear abandonment and thus become overly submissive and dependent, or they may try to control and dominate their partner using guilt and fear."

The woman spoke next. "We also have expectations that we project onto our partners. For instance, we expect our partner to make us happy. This eliminates personal responsibility by placing the burden of happiness onto our partner."

The woman looked at Follin carefully before continuing. "Both males and females have the capacity to control and dominate others emotionally and physically. To manage this we seek to establish boundaries in our relationships. Your lesson in the Cups Kingdom is to learn how to set, enforce and defend your boundaries."

Follin was mentally making notes so that he wouldn't miss anything. He hadn't heard relationships explained in this way before.

"I think I understand that, but why do you want to marry this man?" Follin asked of the woman.

"I wonder if I should tell you, Follin, isn't this the reason you are here? To learn about boundaries?" she replied smartly.

Follin closed his eyes the better to contemplate her question. He saw it as an energy form in front of him, spinning this way and that. Eventually, a pattern began to form and he came back to the couple with his answer.

"You entered this marriage with no expectations of love, thus friendship and affection could grow without enabling those stifling projections you mentioned. By setting boundaries your partner was able to manage his fears of abandonment and thus love flourished."

The young woman smiled brightly. "Well done, Follin. Boundaries reflect the subtle dance of your rational mind and your emotional urges. It is through this dance that you will learn to appreciate the power of the Cups change point."

Chapter 3 – Three of Cups

Celebration, friendship, community, harvest.

As the Storm Chaser arrived at the City of Life, Page Jon explained that unlike the other Tarot Kingdoms the castle of the Cups Kingdom was built under the ocean waves. Follin and Eve leaned over the ship's railing trying to see it as the ship's cargo was unloaded.

"We've never had a war here so we don't need big walls or stone towers," explained Kahmia proudly.

"Is that because you have a special magic that holds back the Wildlanders?" asked Eve. Her own village in the north of the Mystic Isle had borne the brunt of the Wildlander invasions for centuries. She knew plenty about warfare, death and displacement.

"Not at all," said Kahmia. "Our allies in the Tarot Empire protect us."

Follin scratched his head in bewilderment. "But why would they do that? I mean, soldiers get killed, farmers lose their livestock and property is destroyed. Supporting an army is expensive. Warfare uses up massive amounts of resources, so why would the other Kingdoms protect you for free?"

"We help as best we can by patrolling the west coast and the seaways," explained Jon. "Our Dolphin Clan is especially attuned to the oceans and waterways, Sir Rohan leads them." Noticing Follin's frown Jon continued. "The Dolphin Clan aren't people though, they really are dolphins." Follin and Eve's eyes opened wide in astonishment, this was all so strange to them.

Kahmia stepped in to help explain the intricacies of the Cups Kingdom. "Our Kingdom is the largest of the Tarot Empire. We pay homage to those who protect us by providing supplies, medical services and support. We also send our trained healers to help those afflicted by war."

"But why haven't we met many Cups healers on our travels?" asked Eve.

"Oh, you will when you get to the Wands Kingdom, there's plenty up there. You see, Eve, we don't have mages, we have healers. They undergo rigorous training that takes many years to complete. Our mission is to provide hospitals and healing services in each Kingdom of the Empire. We also provide hospices for the displaced and homeless, war veterans and their families, and for those suffering trauma. Setting up these hospices has been one of our greatest accomplishments."

"We've seen hospices but, Kahmia, why so few healers?"

This time Sir Rohan answered. "Healing is a calling, Eve. Those who are called must undergo specialised training that helps them cope with the emotional trauma they are exposed to. We Cups are fragile, more so than the elves we share our blood with. We can't cope with violence. You'll notice that our hospitals are filled with our own disturbed brothers and sisters who turn to alcohol and drugs to cope with the pressures of life and those who fall by the wayside."

Eve and Follin looked around at their friends.

"It's true," said Ziggy. "Elves hide because of their vulnerability to unconstrained human emotions. Cups have inherited those traits and added their own sensitivities."

"We don't have the same robust fortitude as others do in the Empire," explained Sir Rohan. "That's why we spend so much time in meditation and meditating in our backyard pools. Those of us who succeed in managing our emotions are true warriors of the spirit, capable of going into the world to perform feats of courage as healers. They do not buckle under the pressure of stress or trauma, they have learned to go beyond. These are the true masters of the Quest of Life meditation."

"We approach the Quest of Life with great seriousness," continued Jon. "We don't teach outsiders, it is too powerful and might be used for other purposes."

Kahmia looked around at the group to make sure that everyone had finished speaking then she stood and performed a polite bow. "Our dear friends, Eve and Follin. On behalf of our

Cups King and Queen; Sir Rohan, Royal Knight and adept of the Dolphin Clan; Jon and myself, Pages of the Royal family, members of the Royal Merrow; would like to take this opportunity to officially invite you to join us in the Quest of Life ceremony. Would you please honour our Kingdom by accepting this invitation?"

"Thank you," replied Follin taking care to return Kahmia's formal bow. "We would be honoured and delighted to undertake your Quest of Life."

~

The first thing the Pages did was show Follin and Eve their new home. It was a cottage right on the beach. There was a large pond at the back of the house among gardens that provided colour and shade. Eve was excited to see that they could sit and watch the waves crashing on the beach from their front porch each morning.

"This is just stunning," she sighed.

Over the next few weeks, Follin and Eve spent a lot of time at the beach. Whenever they passed groups of Cups swimming among the waves they were encouraged to join in. Although they could swim a little, they'd not had much opportunity to do more than paddle during their childhood on the Mystic Isle.

Once they had settled into their home, Kahmia and Jon showed them how to use their pond. The pond itself was an ecosystem of fish, tortoises, frogs and water plants. One section was kept clear for meditation while the rest was an aquatic haven for the many species that lived there.

"This is where you can meditate in complete peace. No one would think to interrupt you while you are meditating in your pond," explained Kahmia.

In those first weeks, Kahmia took Follin and Eve to visit the city's hospitals and refuges where they learned that the Cups provided healing on many levels: spiritual and emotional as well as physical. Eve was particularly fascinated in these visits and accepted their invitation to lend her healing skills.

"Thank you, I would love to. My parents and grandparents taught me hands-on healing and how to use the herbs from the forest. I also studied herbal medicine with the Pentacles master herbalists, and Mage Hermes is teaching me how to use the astrology chart to aid in diagnosis," she explained. "I would be honoured to be part of your hospital's healing team."

~

Follin and Eve's activities included a combination of swimming and extended deep diving in the sea each morning, then lying on the bottom of their backyard pond later in the day. These exercises were demanding and exhausting - but they were also effective in teaching them to focus their mind and to hold their breath for longer and longer periods.

"Follin," said Sir Rohan one particularly frustrating afternoon. "Water meditation is what initiates the Quest of Life. It is more than holding one's breath, it's learning to breathe 'light' into your body. When you breathe the energy of light you will be able to meld with your wife and breathe as one. When you can do that then the magic happens. The magical part of the quest only comes once you can perform the water breathing. Our water meditation is very passive, one must allow it to happen rather than try to force it."

Each day they would practise their water breathing techniques as they swam and dived to the seabed exploring the reefs and creatures that lived there. As they struggled to the surface gasping for breath the Mystic Islanders swore there was no way they would ever learn to breathe underwater. Exhausted they would crawl out of the surf and lie on the beach to soak up the warm sunshine and recover.

The problem was that none of the Cups knew how to teach water breathing, they had learned it in the womb and so it was second nature to them. The teaching really had to come from an outsider.

~

It was only after some months into their arrival that they found the key to their Quest of Life water breathing exercise.

On that day Sir Darwyn and Ziggy joined them on the beach for a swim. Both men had bodies hardened from years of patrolling with the Elf Rangers, the Pentacles and the Wands Commandos.

"What do you think about this water meditation, Ziggy? You've not swum in the ocean for centuries, how do you remember to breathe underwater?" joked Sir Darwyn after their morning swim.

Ziggy was seated on the sand, his lithe body shining like a bronzed Adonis. The seawater left whitened patches of salt on his skin as he dried in the sun.

"I don't know, I honestly don't. It just comes naturally to..." Ziggy stopped talking to glance over his shoulder. Walking towards them across the sand was a wizened old man carrying a threadbare towel carelessly flung over his shoulder. He was dressed in short pants and wore a tattered straw hat. His almost translucent white legs were a dazzling contrast to the well-tanned group on the beach.

"Hello, I hope I haven't interrupted anything?" The Hierophant's smile was broad and he had a glint of mischief in his eyes.

The old man carefully lay his towel on the sand and sat heavily upon it. He then eased himself onto the towel and pulled his hat over his eyes. When no one moved he propped himself up on one elbow, lifted the edge of his hat and looked around.

"What's taking you so long? Come along, join me in my meditation."

Eve giggled, Follin frowned, and Kahmia and Jon laughed as they lay back on the warm sand to join The Hierophant in his meditation. Even Ziggy and Sir Darwyn closed their eyes in anticipation of another adventure. No one wanted to miss an opportunity to join The Hierophant in a journey to his mystical world.

Follin and Eve could hear The Hierophant's voice guiding them. "You both know the fundamentals of centred breathing from your lessons with The Empress and The High Priestess. The Cups have taken this basic form and adapted it to become a softer meditation, they allow it to flow, just like water. They called it the Quest of Life."

The Hierophant demonstrated by letting them meld with his body. They could feel it as a soft warmth that slowly penetrated deep behind their navel. It pulsed and glowed at the centre of their abdomen. To their amazement, they could feel The Hierophant's slow breathing, in and out, but his lungs remained still - he wasn't breathing at all.

"Your goal is to slow your breath until you feel a subtle pulsation within your body. The fact is that you will eventually be able to breathe a single breath over a period of thirty minutes, at which time you must come up for air. Only those born with this technique can do it for extended periods of time," came The Hierophant's soothing voice.

As if by magic Follin stopped breathing. Concentrating on the pulsing sensation within his mentor's abdomen he sensed a warmth, like air, entering and leaving his navel centre without any effort, without him needing to breathe. Eve sensed her husband's state of focused awareness and automatically synchronised with him. For that brief moment, they were one.

"Ah, there, you can feel it can't you, lovely. Now let me show you one of the many adventures available to you with this Quest of Life meditation. Join me in returning to the moment of your birth." To his Cups friends, Sir Darwyn and Ziggy, he added, "and you lot can come along if you wish, you might learn something." There was a mild chuckle in his voice as they all joined the great man on what would be a memorable adventure.

When Follin and Eve awoke sometime later it was sunset. There was just a hint of coolness in the air as the sky was spreading a blanket of red and orange across the horizon.

"Well, my dears, you now know that you were able to breathe without air before you were born. Do you believe that you can now undertake the Quest of Life?" asked The Hierophant, back in his usual guise of an earthen-brown cloak, leather walking shoes and soft felt hat.

"I think I can do it, yes," Follin replied. "But it made me sad to remember my birth. Why did I feel such sadness to leave my mother's womb?"

"I felt the same thing." Eve leaned on one elbow to stare at The Hierophant. "Such sadness. Does that mean every newborn child feels the grief of separation at birth?"

The Hierophant nodded in understanding. "What you did is unheard of in the world beyond the Cups Kingdom, I might add. Cups are born in water and are gently nurtured through their separation from their mother. I believe it may be much the same for the elven people?"

They all turned to Ziggy, sitting quietly with his legs up and his chin resting on his knees. "I believe so. I wasn't born as such, so I can't honestly say I've had a birthing, not like humans. But when my two children were born," he paused for a moment as a shadow of sadness fleetingly passed across his face before he could suppress it. "My children were birthed by my wife aided by her mother and aunts. I need to explain that Sorcha was a Water Elf and her clan have lived in the water since the beginning of time. They perform a special birthing ritual for months prior to the baby's arrival. It is also our ritual to invite new souls into our homes before they are born. It's nice... it's..." Ziggy stopped and was silent, lost in his own private world.

"Ahem, Follin, I'm quite pleased with how you went, you too, Eve." The Hierophant politely redirected the conversation away from Ziggy. He looked at the two lovers. "The Quest of Life is a water style of energy breathing, it is similar to what you learned from Frailbones when he did his healing meditation with you, Follin. Eve, you did a similar technique when healing Mondy and

Natalie in your trek to the Swords Kingdom. All you need do is slowly and gently breathe water energy into your navel centre, you don't stop until you are completely full. Once you are charged you simply let go. You will no longer need to breathe for a period of time. When you run out of oxygen you simply go back to doing more soft, gentle breathing. With practice, this period of 'no breath' will last longer and longer."

The Hierophant stopped talking when he realised that the sun had set and they were alone on the beach. "Come on, if I don't stop talking now I'll keep you here until midnight. Let's get back to the cottage and have something to eat."

On their return to the cottage, Follin walked over to Ziggy and gently touched his arm.

"I'm sorry you had to remember." Follin could feel his friend's sorrow deep in his own heart.

"It is all right, Follin. I was caught unawares that's all. I know I should talk about my feelings, but elf folk are proud folk, we don't talk to others about our problems." Ziggy put his hand on Follin's shoulder. "When you've completed your Quest of Life I'd like you to come with me, to visit my people, the Daru Clan of the Wood Elves."

"But, Ziggy, I'm not an elf. I, I don't know if I am allowed to visit your sacred elven places," stuttered Follin. "I'm just the son of a common mage who ran away from home."

Ziggy turned to Follin. "Elf-wise, there is something important for you to do there, as have I." The elf stared into Follin's grey eyes. "I have felt the threads of destiny binding us together. Please trust me, for trust is sometimes all we have."

~

The day of their Quest Of Life finally arrived. The entire city was up early, some of the were even celebrating in the streets. Many more were at the beach waiting for their Mystic Isle visitors to arrive for their quest with the King and Queen. Although quite anxious, Follin and Eve looked forward to this unusual initiation. The Hierophant was dressed formally as were Follin and Eve. They were escorted to the ocean's edge by Pages Jon and Kahmia.

"What do we do now?" asked Eve. This was a very special celebration and she wasn't quite sure what to expect.

"You don't need to do anything, Eve. It's exactly the same as how we trained every day. Just start your water breathing then walk into the water. Allow the waves to do the rest. Don't worry, we'll guide you to the Water Castle." The Hierophant took each by the hand and slowly walked them into the ocean waves.

It was easier than they expected. The very first wave drew them down into its ocean home. Follin found himself swimming with his friends towards the Water Castle as though he was flying in the air. He sensed Eve beside him, their breathing already in synchrony. The Water Castle was much the same as the castles Follin and Eve had seen in the Pentacles and Swords Kingdoms. The entryway was through a stone arch where the wedding group were met and escorted to the main throne room.

"Welcome to our Cups Castle, dear cousins. We are honoured to offer you union in the Quest of Life." The voice was delivered telepathically by the stately gentleman seated on his throne, the King of Cups.

Beside him sat the Queen who hurriedly smoothed her gown which kept creeping upwards drawn by the currents twisting and tangling everything that wasn't firmly secured. She laughed gaily, "I knew I should have worn my tight evening dress, these formal gowns just don't want to cooperate."

"My dear," said the King. "You look lovely no matter what you wear. But shall we begin the quest? We don't want to use up the newcomers' air in trivial conversation now do we." The King acknowledged the other guests: The Emperor and his wife, The Empress; High Priestess Hera fading almost to invisibility; Hermes the Magician; The Hierophant; Sir Darwyn and Ziggy the elf.

The Queen ordered her staff to close the doors. Once that small task was completed the ceremony began.

"We, the Royal Merrow of the Cups Kingdom, bear witness to the initiation of Follin and Eve, of the Mystic Isle, into the Quest of Life," announced the King. "The quest binds husband and wife in a synchrony of mind, body and spirit to create a single soul."

"This is a small gathering, yet I hear the Cups community above await your completion of the quest so that they can celebrate in the traditional manner," announced the Queen who, once more, had to gather her gown as it sought to encircle herself and the King. "This is not a wedding ceremony, it is an initiation into the secrets of life itself. We do not offer this quest lightly, and I know that you have studied and practised with great respect. Yet I wish to emphasise its incredible power, a power that comes with enormous responsibility. The Quest of Life is not just the uniting of souls and the ritual sharing of seaweed wine," the Queen laughed lightly as she saw Eve's face twist in disgust. "It is to reward your efforts in learning something beyond normal human capability."

The King explained. "The water breathing technique, which is necessary to undertake the Quest of Life, involves breathing the very essence that pervades the universe. This technique opens a doorway into dimensions beyond our own. The quest opens the practitioner to alternate planes of existence, however, very few practitioners are able to access even a small part of the spectrum that it makes available."

The Emperor spoke next. "This particular meditation form led us to discover planet Earth and is the force behind the Quest of Life. It enabled us to speak with Pan, the creator of this beautiful planet. The opening of your centre of power at your navel was my wife's responsibility, Follin. The Cups' Quest of Life, is an adjunct meditation that can lead you to other worlds, and other adventures."

The King of Cups invited everyone to hold hands forming a circle around the table. His aura glowed brighter until everyone glowed with a power that engulfed Follin and Eve. "It is our honour to take you on a journey which will help answer some of your questions, and no doubt pose many new ones."

The universe spun and Follin suddenly felt Eve as part of his own consciousness. As one they saw star systems and their inhabitants, they watched as various species evolved and changed in consciousness as well as form.

A voice narrated the events as they watched: "Please focus, for this is where we came from." An image of a planetary system orbiting a star passed in front of his gaze. They next saw the Milky Way and then planet Earth circling a similar star, Sol. "That is the planet we are now inhabiting. Each planetary system has different rules of existence. This one, the Sol System, is particularly aligned with cause and effect."

That must be why The Empress kept reminding me – what comes around goes around,' Follin thought.

"Exactly," came the reply.

They could see a world of green leaves and rich soil, the environment was very similar to Earth's.

"That is where we came from, the Tarot origins," offered another voice which sounded like The Empress. "It was a beautiful world where we sought spiritual perfection just as a plant ascends to seek the light. We had to leave when the acts of our less enlightened brothers and sisters caused the atmosphere to become so toxic that it threatened the survival of all living beings."

Follin could hear the sadness in the voice and realised that the Tarot Empire evolved on a beautiful planet. *'I wonder why it grew so toxic?'* he asked himself.

Another voice answered. "Our star system was old and our people ruthless in their greed to indulge in physical pleasures. We were but a small band of spiritual seekers wishing to find a deeper meaning to our existence. We found this within our soul but time had run out and we were forced to evolve in haste before our planet died. The Emperor discovered the meditation which you are experiencing now."

Many hours later Follin slowly awoke on the beach. The tide had gone out and he was sitting on the dry sand in the same place as when he had begun his quest. He felt buoyant and happy, more alive than he had felt for a long time. It was late afternoon but the crowd had remained, quietly waiting for the couple's return.

At first, he was confused not quite knowing who he was. *'Am I Follin or am I Eve?'* he thought. But there, sitting beside him, was his wife, Eve, with Sox lying between them, one eye open, watching them carefully. Soon other members of their party joined them. Escorted by hundreds of dancing and singing Cups they were ready to celebrate their initiation in the Quest of Life.

~

Follin's Meditation - Three of Cups

A few nights after their quest, Follin was ready to explore the next picture in his possession. The image showed three young maidens each holding a cup raised above their heads as they danced. The girls appeared to be having a celebration of some kind. At their feet lay a selection of fruits and vegetables from the harvest. Without making any effort Follin allowed himself to enter the image with the dancing girls.

"Hello," he called. "Please don't stop, I can see you are enjoying yourselves." Watching the girls dancing he could feel their sensual movements deep within his body. It aroused his life force which made him think that it was a fertility dance.

"Indeed it is," said the first girl and she stepped lightly over to him. The young woman smiled seductively as she caressed his face with the tips of her fingers. "Fertility begins with arousal, and then, with a burst of ecstasy, the seed is implanted with life. For nine months the fruit is nurtured within before it is ready for harvest."

The second girl walked over and pulled her sister's hand away. "Sister, this young man is wed, can you not see? He has performed the sacred Quest of Life and is bound by his virtue to honour and respect his partner. None of us will succeed in extracting his pollen to fertilise our flowers."

The third girl laughed drawing Follin's attention.

"Follin, don't let my sisters tease you, we have a gift for you and Eve. It is a gift that will take long months to bear fruit." In her hand, she held what appeared to be an egg. She seductively flounced her curvaceous body over to Follin and with her fingers she closed his eyes. "Follin, will you do us the honour of accepting our gift?"

At that moment Sox's bark broke into his consciousness. He gently drew the girl's fingers apart to see Sox looking at him, prompting for his master to accept the gift. Behind Sox, he could see Molly, the blind elemental. She had a broad smile on her face. He recognised that the girl's gift was honourably given and there was no malice nor trick attached to it. He allowed the girl's fingers to cover his eyes again.

"Sisters, I gratefully accept your gift and respectfully look forward to its fruit when the time is right for its picking." He suddenly felt something warm and soothing pressed into his abdomen, just below his navel.

"With this gift, you will be blessed beyond you and your wife's wildest expectations. Go softly, go gently, dear Follin."

With some difficulty, Follin awoke from his meditation. The sun was soon to rise and he could feel Eve stirring beside him. As she sleepily turned to face him an urgent need to unite consumed them.

Chapter 4 – Four of Cups

Sadness, withdrawal, avoiding a situation, reflection.

Once they had completed the Quest of Life, Follin and Eve had time to relax and enjoy the pleasures of their new home. Each morning they awoke to the soothing sound of waves breaking on the sandy beach in front of their cottage. They would leisurely rise to enjoy a light breakfast in the front garden overlooking the ocean, then spend the rest of the day with their friends. It was so peaceful that they thought their mentors had all but forgotten them. When the Archetypes did visit it was simply to enjoy their company.

"I don't get it," grunted Follin one morning. "We've been studying every day and night ever since we arrived in the Empire, but now, as soon as we've completed this quest, they leave us alone. I don't know what to think of it."

Eve quietly sipped at her mug of coffee while watching the seagulls dive on a school of poddy mullet close to shore. Kahmia had a thing for coffee and often brought a batch of her fresh roasted beans over for Eve to try. Follin wasn't impressed, it was too bitter for his taste, he stuck to his usual cup of black tea. 'Coffee,' he would say, 'tastes like burnt toast.'

"Love, remember what the King said at the end of our quest? He said that one day we will fly to the stars. So don't worry, they'll call on us if they think we're getting lazy."

"I'm a bit disappointed though. Mage Hermes had just started showing me how to interpret transits to the natal chart too. I suppose I can practice astrology by myself, but... hey, maybe they're giving us a holiday?" offered Follin, spreading a thick layer of honey on the freshly baked bread delivered by one of their generous neighbours. "Oh yeah, Eve, I just remembered. Did I tell you that Ziggy wants to take me to his Wood Elf village?"

"No, what did Ziggy say?" replied Eve looking up from her breakfast of barley and oat porridge. Follin had raved about the joys of porridge so much that she had decided to give it a try - and loved it. He said that it was basically all he could afford to eat for the seven years of his sojourn with the Tarot Major Arcana.

"Ziggy hinted that he had some healing of his own to do." Follin paused as he struggled to remember exactly what his elf friend had told him.

"You've forgotten haven't you!" laughed Eve, teasing her husband. "Did Ziggy say if Sir Darwyn was going as well? Those two spend all their spare time together. I think they've spent hundreds if not thousands of years as friends. They almost talk the same don't they."

It was Follin's turn to laugh. "Yes, they are similar, but Sir Darwyn is always happy while Ziggy, well, there's always a sadness about him." This time Follin stopped talking because he had seen in his friend's memories why he experienced these episodes of melancholy.

Eve could tell Follin was holding back and was curious. "Well? What is it? You've not told me everything have you," she said.

Follin felt trapped. He had a secret but he didn't like to keep secrets from Eve, it didn't feel right. Besides, now that he had brought it into consciousness she could mind-read him if she wanted, all she had to do was start her water breathing.

"Well, Ziggy did say he was once married and had two children but they were taken from him. I have a feeling something bad happened to them, that's all," he finally admitted.

Eve nodded, she'd heard much the same, it wasn't news to her. She decided to change the subject to avoid upsetting Follin. He was sensitive about things to do with family and children, perhaps because of what happened in his own childhood.

"How about we call Molly and Sox and go down to the beach and play?"

Follin grinned, quickly finished his toast and stood ready to find Sox. Just as he took that first step to fetch his fae dog, Follin noticed a sudden shift in the energy fields of the Empire.

"Hey, what just happened, Eve?"

Eve tapped her chest and shuddered. "I felt it too, here inside me. It's like nothing I've experienced before. I saw Hera, too, she was..." Eve paused shifting her eyes from side to side searching for a suitable word. "Hera looked... trapped. I've not seen her like this before. I must go to her, now."

~

The Empress arrived at the Sanctuary within minutes. What she saw shocked her. It was a shambles and Hera was nowhere to be seen. With a sharp intake of breath, she saw that the beautiful plant life and groomed gardens were already wilting as if they had been poisoned.

"Oh, no!" The Empress cried in panic. "What is happening? The Sanctuary is dying!"

In her meditation Eve saw The Empress' hand go to her face and she too let out a gasp of horror.

"What is happening, Eve?" cried The Empress, her voice tight with dread as she sensed Eve remote viewing the Sanctuary. "I felt something horrid just happen and knew it must be the Sanctuary, but this is awful."

There was a litter of dead birds spread across one of the grassy glades of the Sanctuary. The Empress raced across the parched grass to scoop one in her hands. It was clear that no amount of magic would revive it.

"What is happening here? Where is Hera?"

"The pond, look!" cried Eve, now seeing the murky, scum covered pond. Dead fish floated on its surface and she sensed the smell of decay in the air.

At that moment a nearby tree cracked in warning just before it crashed to the ground. The Empress had to run to avoid its falling branches. It was clear that the roots were rotten and the open soil smelled like a suppurating wound.

"This can't be happening," moaned The Empress. "Only a few days ago Hera was all smiles. The Sanctuary's integrity is corrupted, it's caused the Tarot Empire's delicate state of harmony to destabilise, this is so wrong."

"We knew that the Sanctuary was a little out of balance, but the High Priestess and Mage Hermes have been keeping an eye on it. I'll ask Molly to find out what's happening, maybe she can advise us." Eve sat quietly, eased her breathing to slow even further and called for Molly.

"Good idea, Eve, I'll call in Temperance and the Star Lady," said The Empress as she found a seat by the pond and forced herself to relax. "The angels helped create the Sanctuary in the very early days, they may know what to do." The Empress was silent for a moment, then continued. "The Kings and Queens of each Kingdom have joined us, they're all linked to the Sanctuary too. They're doing everything they can to engage their elemental magic to help."

When Eve connected with her elemental, she noticed that Molly was frozen, shivering in fear. She had never seen her like this before.

"Molly?" she said, "are you going to be all right?"

"I'll be fine, just give me a moment. It is the energy here, it stinks!" Molly indicated for Eve to extend her aura so that she could borrow some of her energy. This was a difficult and dangerous task. When The Empress sensed what Molly was doing she opened her own aura for Molly to use.

"I feel it, Eve, I can feel it," whispered The Empress. "The Wildlander mages have done this. They deliberately distracted Hera so that they could send a disruptive energy form into the Sanctuary. The Sanctuary has no protection against this strange type of magic. I don't know if we can shift it in time to save the Empire."

~

"Follin?" called a familiar voice. "Follin!" Its urgency caused Follin to turn abruptly. The Hierophant stood in the doorway of the cottage swaying slightly. The tension emanating from the old man was palpable.

"Follin, we have a crisis on our hands. I've called our friends to join us, they'll be here soon." When Follin went to waken Eve from her meditation The Hierophant put his hand on his shoulder. "Leave her, she's busy with The Empress." Follin could feel The Hierophant's hand shaking.

"It's the Sanctuary, there's something really bad happening in the Sanctuary, isn't there?" Follin asked, his lips quivered for a second before he could control himself.

The Hierophant took a slow, deep breath before answering. "Yes, and it's serious. The Sanctuary has been attacked and Hera has disappeared. The Empress has sent for the Angels who helped create the Sanctuary, and each of the Kingdom's Kings and Queens are engaged at an elemental level to try and stop the situation worsening."

Follin could detect uncertainty in The Hierophant's voice. "It really is bad isn't it," he mumbled, his voice faltering. He well knew that the two Angel Archetypes, Temperance and the Star Lady, had created it, along with the very first High Priestess, specifically to protect and nurture the Tarot Empire.

"This just isn't fair. Eve and I have hardly begun to enjoy each other's company and this has to happen!" Follin put his hands to his face and rubbed them back and forth. His face was wet, he hadn't realised just how much he had been perspiring.

"Nothing is 'fair', Follin, you should know that!" retorted The Hierophant sharply. "There is only perpetual vigilance. The mystic doesn't complain he simply continues his daily exercises and performs the right and proper actions regardless of fairness." The Hierophant sat down with a loud, "harrumph!" and poured himself a cup of tea. He was so not himself that he manifested both teapot and cup out of thin air.

There came voices from the front of the house. Recognising his friends, Follin called to let the visitors know to come through to the kitchen where he and The Hierophant were sitting. Ziggy and Sir Darwyn stopped when they saw The Hierophant's far-away look.

"Master Hierophant, are you feeling all right?" asked Sir Darwyn softly.

The old man seemed more wizened than ever. He sat silently peering through the window at the waves on the beach, his cup of tea held motionless in his right hand. He appeared to be frozen. Sox nudged the old man's leg several times before putting his chin on The Hierophant's knee - but The Hierophant remained as silent and still as a statue.

Sir Darwyn spoke to the two men beside him. "It's OK, he's pondering the situation at the Sanctuary. He won't go there, not now, not while the girls are doing their work. He is trying to locate the problem. If he can he'll put a stop to the rot."

"Rot?" asked Follin in s soft voice.

"Yes," replied The Charioteer. "Something has happened to the Sanctuary and Hera has disappeared, she isn't there to guard it anymore."

Ziggy too had slipped into a light trance leaving Follin wondering whether he should do the same, though he wasn't sure what he could do to help. Some moments later Ziggy returned to full consciousness, visibly subdued.

"Hera has been injured in some way," he announced to his friends. "The energy of the Wildlander mages has infiltrated the Sanctuary. It's a form of energy I've not seen before."

As Ziggy finished speaking, The Hierophant came back from his trance. The tortured look on his face said it all.

"They have taken Hera and no one can locate her," he said woodenly.

~

"Eve," called The Empress. "We need you to help us manage and defend the Sanctuary for a while. The magic that has done this has completely blocked me. Tarot magic is useless, but whatever has done this might not notice Molly's elemental magic. I need her to find the change point and bring the Sanctuary back into some sort of balance."

"I must return to my body to help Molly, Empress."

The Empress needed Eve to be physically present in the Sanctuary itself. *'I really need Eve here in the Sanctuary. I must speak with The Hierophant about this,'* she thought.

When Eve returned to her body in the cottage by the sea, she suddenly felt her energy shift again. "Molly, I can feel the change point! Quickly do something before the Sanctuary completely collapses!"

Within moments there came a sighing sound and a release of tension. It was like a cool breeze blowing through the Sanctuary's flowers and tall trees. A surge of vitality sprang into Eve's awareness, the Sanctuary was coming back to life.

The Empress suddenly looked around the gardens and wiped her brow. "She did it," she sighed. "Molly found the change point. That was quite an amazing thing for Eve's elemental to do."

As pleased as The Empress was, Eve had frozen, at her feet lay Molly. Her little friend didn't move. Bending down Eve gently lifted the blind mole to her breast, she could feel her elemental's life-force slowly ebbing away in her grasp.

She let out a frightening scream, "Somebody! Please do something! Molly is dying!"

~

The Hierophant turned at Eve's scream and saw her clutching the still form of her courageous elemental in her lap. Molly had exhausted her energy and was disintegrating, evolving backwards, back to the elemental void from which she had come. The Hierophant immediately engaged his archetypal form and gently took Molly from Eve's shaking hands. He found Molly's life force at the core of her being and held it, thus preventing her from spiralling into oblivion.

Eve sat exhausted, powerless to do more than watch as The Hierophant breathed his life-force into Molly's body. With a sudden lurch, the elemental mole awoke and opened her eyes. She turned towards Eve and beckoned to be given to her mistress. Once in Eve's arms, she curled herself into a furry ball and fell into a deep healing sleep.

"That little elemental of yours is a wonder," The Hierophant said softly, exhaustion sitting on the edge of his voice. "She bravely sought the change point despite the enormous danger of the Wildlander's corrosive magic. Somehow she managed to shift it back to where it should be, but it nearly cost the poor creature her life." Turning to his friends gathered around him, he said, "I think we now have a small window of opportunity to make our way to the Emperor's castle to rescue Hera. We must consolidate the adjustments Molly has made to the change point."

Ziggy looked at Eve, then at The Hierophant and said, "I'm in, my people will help too."

Follin immediately put his hand up and nodded to the Hierophant, "You'll need someone to hold your horses while you rescue the High Priestess, so count me in too."

Ziggy glanced side-ways at Follin and smiled. "We would not think of leaving without you, elf-wise. Nor do I think your use limited to holding our horse's reins."

Follin smiled brightly, this was high praise indeed. He went over and sat beside Eve putting his arm around her shoulder. She snuggled into him and closed her eyes, Molly clutched tightly to her breast - it had been a stressful morning.

The Charioteer, still grinning at Ziggy and Follin's exchange, turned to the tired old man sitting with his elbow on the table, a fresh cup of tea clutched tightly in his fist. "You will need someone with brains and good looks to participate in a mission as dangerous as this. Count me in as well."

Sox had been watching the men talking. Recognising where their conversation was heading he raced into Follin's room to bring out his sword in its scabbard. The fae dog dropped it at his master's feet then returned with his quiver of arrows. Finally, he brought Follin's precious Bowman's bow.

"Lad, I think Sox wants us to stop talking and start moving," chuckled Ziggy, standing to adjust the long knife in his belt. He swung it to the small of his back, all the better for running. "Darwyn and I will be back in a minute, we've our fighting and travelling gear in our cottage. We'll send one of the stable boys to bring our horses." With that Ziggy and Sir Darwyn raced out of the cottage.

"Follin," said The Hierophant. "I need you to call on Sir Rohan and Page Jon. I believe the answer may be found with the aid of their Water Elf cousins. We will meet them on our way to the Emperor's castle."

~

Follin's Meditation - Four of Cups

The picture showed a seated man who appeared depressed or perhaps he was melancholic or irritated, Follin felt it hard to decide just what emotion was on display here. Standing upright at the man's feet were three cups while another was handed to him from a puff of smoke or mist. The moment Follin began his meditation he was drawn into the body of the man in the picture.

'Is he drunk?' was Follin's first thought.

"I was promised so much but so little eventuated, I feel betrayed and lost. Why promise something and not deliver?" Follin could feel the man's sense of betrayal and abandonment.

'I've got to get out of this man's body,' Follin said to himself as he began to feel melancholic himself.

As he turned away Follin studied the mist with its disembodied hand grasping a cup. It was reaching towards the man as though in offering to ease the man's depression, yet the man failed to see it.

Follin applied his Swords lesson of clarity and examined the situation closely. 'Aha, this man had high expectations yet when only part of his desire came into actuality he felt rejected, disappointed, betrayed and abandoned.' Follin remembered his own feelings as a youngster in the man's disappointment.

'That's what the other pictures have been saying to me: identify and manage my feelings before they overtake me. So many lessons yet they are so appropriate for what I'm experiencing right now. I've gone to bed disappointed that Eve and I had our honeymoon cut short by the crisis in the Sanctuary. I felt alone yet now everyone has come together to join us in rescuing

Hera. I feel the unity of friendship and camaraderie in this frightful situation. I can't feel abandoned when there is such a supportive community here, and I am part of it.'

Follin eased himself from the man's image to return to his own body. He wrote up his journal and then fell asleep.

Chapter 5 – Five of Cups
Pain of loss, new bridges to cross.

With the blessing of the King and Queen of Cups, Follin and Eve set off on their journey to the Tarot Empire's Sanctuary with the mixed band of Archetypes, Wood Elf and Cups royalty. The sun was shining but the wind was blowing from the north portending a wet ride to the Emperor's castle.

"Hey, Darwyn!" called Sir Rohan, a smile playing across his face. "Where's your chariot, we might need it if one of our horses become lame."

"It's in for repairs with the Pentacles wagoneers," replied Sir Darwyn a little stiffly. "I damaged it in the Hindamar Mountains on patrol with the Elf Rangers and the Pentacles Mountaineers. How was I supposed to know I might need it to rescue the High Priestess?"

It was only a few hours into their trip before a light rain began to fall. As they walked their horses along the muddying paths that wound towards the Emperor's castle, the group discussed the situation and possible solutions. When they stopped to put their oilskin coats on the conversation turned towards the main question - why did Hera allow strange magic into the Sanctuary?

"How can an Archetype like Hera get tricked like that?" asked Page Jon of The Hierophant as he climbed into his wet saddle.

The Hierophant nodded his head up and down sending drips of water down the back of his coat as he considered the question. "I've been asking myself the same question, Jon. All I can think of is that Hera was caught in some kind of enchantment, like a spiders web."

Jon wouldn't be put off by such a simplistic answer. "But she is an Archetype, the most powerful there is, isn't she? And she must know that she is imprisoned right now, wouldn't she?"

Again The Hierophant's head bobbed up and down as he considered his reply. "For your information, Hera was born on Runda Isle, she is Mage Hermes's twin sister. The Emperor and Empress made her an Archetype when she accepted her role as High Priestess. Perhaps that has something to..."

"And where's Mage Hermes, he should be here with us helping the Empire," Jon butted in. The exhausted Archetype was trying to find an answer to their dilemma, something he normally would do with ease, but today was very different - The Hierophant felt defeated.

"Jon, I don't know where he is. All I know is that he is on a special mission for The Emperor to save the Sanctuary," replied The Hierophant clearly exasperated with the Page's questions.

The Charioteer came to The Hierophant's rescue. "I think Hera was tricked into letting a cleverly disguised form of rogue energy violate the Sanctuary. I can only guess that a new form of Wildlander magic was used. It tricked her into letting it in and trapped her, or perhaps it has transported her away somewhere." Sir Darwyn looked across his horse's neck at Jon before continuing. "As for Mage Hermes, he's busy trying to find a solution to the problem."

Jon still wasn't satisfied. "That doesn't explain how it happened, Sir Darwyn. Wouldn't Hera run tests or something like that before letting strange magic into the Sanctuary?"

"Jon, we just don't know what happened," grunted The Hierophant. He was clearly annoyed with the Page and his endless questions. "All we have is speculation and at this stage, it is idle speculation at best!"

Jon felt he was being more than reasonable and the rebuke was totally unwarranted. The Cups Page sank into his saddle and dropped to the back of the group to sulk.

"Jon?" Follin called slowing his horse to walk beside his friend. He had missed the conversation and didn't notice his friend's miserable look. "I need some advice."

"What about?" grunted Jon, still somewhat peeved.

"I've been wrestling with something. The lion in my 2 of Cups meditation said I needed to learn the Cups change point and Sir

Rohan said I had to learn about the Cups extreme emotions. I understand the Pentacles and Swords change points but the Cups is too hard. I fear it's beyond me."

Jon stared at his friend for a moment as he settled himself into a more positive mood. "I'm not sure I can answer this as well as Rohan, he spent twenty years in exile learning about the Cups and its change point. I'd say he is the expert, but I'll try my best."

Follin stared at his friend, this was news to him. "I'd no idea Sir Rohan had been exiled. Do you mean that he was banished from his own Kingdom?" When Jon nodded, Follin shook his head in amazement. "Why would a Knight of the Royal Family, the Dolphin Clan leader too, be banished from the Kingdom that he would one day inherit as its King?"

Jon took a few moments before replying. "The answer to that question is best left to the right time and place. Besides, I still need to answer your first question."

At this point, Sox barked at his master.

"See, even Sox knows this is important." Jon was smiling openly now, his bad mood forgotten. "You see, Follin, Cups people are moody and emotional, we swing from one extreme to another, there's hardly any middle ground for us. The change point is within, once you learn to manage your own change point you can possibly, just possibly, help others manage theirs." He paused to let this sink in. "Recognise your feelings, cherish them, nice feelings are precious in a world as hard and dispassionate as this. At the same time recognise the reality of your situation. People are irrational and often delusional when caught in our socially sanctioned web of greed, apathy, love and lust. Learn to view situations from all perspectives within yourself and you will be able to swing the balance to the centre. This is what you might call 'managing the change point'. Cups are trained from birth to be mindful of their messy moods, but sadly, most of us fail. We are vulnerable to our feelings and are easily overwhelmed by them."

Follin nodded. "I sort of get it, Jon, but maybe I'll understand it better when you tell me the story of Sir Rohan's banishment."

~

Their journey took them past market gardens and fields of grain that stretched for miles. As they approached the first field of wheat Follin spied an old, battered scarecrow. He recalled how he had once swapped his own shirt for that of another weathered scarecrow many years earlier. He smiled to himself, *'I was so young and naive back then. I am amazed that I've survived those troubled years.'*

The region they were travelling through was famous for its barley, fresh garden vegetables and its dark ale. On the first night of their trek, they stayed at a tavern in one of the farming villages along the Pilgrim's Way. Jon explained that each year many Cups families would embark on a pilgrimage to visit their Water Elf cousin's hot springs and mud baths for healing and spiritual respite. Arranged at the more famous springs were a number of shrines. These shrines were placed there by the grateful parents of children who had been struck down by plague or disease and had recovered. To provide for these pilgrims, numerous taverns had sprung up to accommodate them. Each was separated by an easy day's walk. These walking paths had spread out like a spiders web right across the Cups Kingdom leading to the Water Elf's healing mud bogs.

The afternoon of their second day they came to the first of the low foothills and small streams that heralded their approach to the elf forests. The lands to the north and west of the City of Life was inhabited by Water Elves, their close kin who affectionately call their Cups cousins 'Merrow' - 'people of the water'. As they entered the forest a small band of elves met them.

"Hail, Ziggy," called a tall, middle-aged elf. He was dressed in forest green with hat and boots of soft leather. There was a long knife in a sheath at his waist, a yew bow and quiver of arrows. In his hand he held a leafy oak branch which, as befit custom, he offered to his cousin in greeting.

"Hail, Ardler. It has been a while since we last met," replied Ziggy as he accepted the branch.

"Hail to my cousins, Rohan and Jon, the blessings of our race to thee." He bowed low to Sir Darwyn and The Hierophant then addressed Follin and Eve. "Hail and welcome, Follin, and your elf-wise wife, Eve."

Follin returned the elf's pleasant smile. He was similar in build to Ziggy – tall and thin with handsome features.

"Hail and well met to you, Master Ardler," replied the two Mystic Islanders.

After greetings had been exchanged and the group had continued along their path, Follin reined in his horse to walk beside the Water Elf.

"Ardler, if you don't mind, I'd like to walk with you and ask some questions that have been on my mind. I've been dying to know more about the differences between the races of the Tarot Empire."

"The path narrows a little further up, why don't you hop down off your horse and walk with me." Ardler helped Follin from his horse then began his explanation. "As you can see, Water Elves no longer live in the rivers or beside the seas as we did in the past. We now live most of our lives in these forests and in the boglands in the west."

A series of squeaks from leather saddles interrupted their conversation as their companions also climbed from their horses. The path had narrowed and they had to continue in single file through the thickening forest.

The rain had stopped but the track was soon churned into a clinging, muddy mess. Sox trotted happily beside his master only to race into the forest to explore at every sound or movement. Sox always came back when Follin put his mind into the void and called him. There were no more games, however, he still enjoyed his time with the many elementals he met on his adventures but was just as excited to return to his master.

Ardler stopped talking to greet a band of similarly armed elf scouts passing on their way to patrol the hills to the west. Ziggy had slowly edged closer to Follin recognising that Ardler's conversation was of great interest to his friend.

"Follin, with the coming of the Tarot Empire the elves changed. Some intermarried which brought about changes in both elf and the Tarot people. Ardler's Water Elf clan intermarried with the Cups not long after the elementals were released from their dream state." Ziggy paused, he watched as Follin digested the information.

"Can you please tell me more about the elementals?" Follin asked.

"Certainly. When Pan created the Earth he placed certain energy beings in special places so that they would awaken at different times in the planet's evolution." Ziggy stopped as the three led their horses around a precarious rocky outcrop, then continued his lesson. "With the coming of the Tarot folk the elementals were awakened early. That's why they are so rare and so powerful, they never fully formed into solid creatures like you and me. They came from the inner world and that's why they can cross the borders to the outer world when they want."

Ardler took up the conversation. "The common link between Water Elves and Cups people is that we all wish to avoid conflict. Elves are strong and robust, they fiercely protect their lands and can be quite violent, like your Mystic Isle elves."

"You are absolutely right there, Ardler, our Mystic Isle elves are ferocious," agreed Follin. "They won't allow us into their forests, especially at certain times of the year when they hold their sacred ceremonies. We do trade with them, though, so they aren't always aggressive. They've been known to kill if we disrespect their customs and taboos though."

"Like those in the Mystic Isle, some elves are quick to temper. Others, like us, would rather weave an invisibility spell than do harm." Having finished his lesson Ardler smiled to Follin and Ziggy and moved silently towards the front of the group.

"Ziggy?" asked Follin. "Is there a difference between your clan and Ardler's?"

"My people, the Wood Elves, are in regular contact with the Tarot and Wildlander folk. Sometimes it leads to confrontation over food, land and security. You heard from Frailbones what happened with my sister, Naroo? That sort of thing has been going on since

Wildlanders decided that they wanted our lands. Ardler's clan avoid conflict by staying hidden in this small forest, tucked away between the peaceful Cups and the rest of the Empire. They have the luxury of a secure home, but most other elves don't."

"If the Water Elves don't like to fight, why did we just see armed elf scouts heading out to patrol the forests?"

Ziggy's face glowed with pride for his kin. "The Water Elves patrol their borders as do we. If they need to fight they will. Don't be fooled by Ardler, his clan are ferocious fighters when they have to be."

~

When the band arrived at the Water Elf village the people flocked to welcome Follin, Eve and Sox. Fae animals were extremely rare, and Sox not only had powers similar to that of elves, he was also Follin's ally, and they all knew that there was something special about Follin.

Ardler rubbed Sox behind the ears. "Carlia has agreed to help you find High Priestess Hera." Eve smiled with relief as Ardler called to his wife.

"Follin and Eve," announced Ardler, "this is my wife, Carlia."

Carlia was similarly dressed, her clothing was as soft as silk and the colour of the forests that surrounded them. Her smile was warm and she had a calming presence. "So, you are both elf-wise? But of course, I can see it. Ziggy has named you. Eve, don't worry, I'm confident that together we shall find a way to rescue your High Priestess."

~

That evening the visitors were seated at a meeting with the Water Elf elders. It was decided that Carlia should lead them in trying to locate High Priestess Hera.

Carlia took Eve by the hand. "Tonight I shall call upon you and your elemental, Molly. I know that she has been exposed to dangerous forces when she balanced the Sanctuary's change point, but I believe that she is well enough to participate in this meditation. She has the support of my clan and we will protect her." Carlia spoke softly, reassuring Eve that her elemental would be in no danger.

Wanting Molly to recover, Eve had not called upon her elemental throughout the trip, but at mention of her name the elemental suddenly appeared in her mistress' lap.

In explanation of what happened in the Sanctuary, Molly said, "I had a fright, as you humans would say, but I trust Carlia. The elves have powers I understand. Relax, Eve, let me do my work."

"Follin, you are here as you are bonded to Sox. Along with Molly, Sox's presence will help us find Hera. Eve, it is you who will walk with me, please, stay focused on my instructions." The elders now closed their eyes and joined Carlia in her meditation.

As Carlia spoke Eve could feel herself fading from the corporeal world to enter the sacred inner world of the elves. Within moments she saw eyes, watching, soft eyes, kind eyes that wished them well.

A voice floated into Eve's mind, 'Welcome, elf-wise, we are here to help you.'

As Eve relaxed into a deeper trance, she saw faces behind the eyes. They were a mixture of elf and fae eyes. Still holding

Carlia's hand she felt herself entering a large cave. Her guide told her to open her eyes. Before her Eve saw a pool of clear water, its surface perfectly smooth. There were neither ripples nor movement on its surface of any kind. Opposite to where Carlia indicated for Eve to sit, was a lighted candle, its reflection on the surface of the pool was clear and bright.

Carlia commanded softly, "Eve, watch the candle's reflection. Soon a drop will fall from the stalactites above. As ripples erupt from its splash I want you to use your mind to bring it back to the same smooth surface as it is now."

Eve found that she had automatically synchronised her breathing with Molly, Follin and Sox. It felt as though she was wrapped in a warm glow of happiness and security. As she sat watching the pool, a water-droplet fell from a long, needle-shaped stalactite above to hit the pool's mirror surface. It caused an eruption of movement. The small waves raced from the centre of the pool to its outer edges. The candle's reflection was scattered, it was impossible for Eve to calm it to its previous flat surface.

"Calm your mind and it will calm the pool surface," came Carlia's soft voice within Eve's mind.

Now Eve could feel Molly's power. When the drops fell it was Molly's mind that forced Eve to focus and remain calm. Soon the two fell into a rhythm. Both Eve and her elemental were operating as a single entity to calm the ripples. Follin was also synchronised in mind and spirit, he did as much as he could to help.

As the pool surface calmed, Carlia brought a thought-form into the meditation - it was of the High Priestess Hera.

"Molly," commanded the elf, "find The High Priestess Hera."

To Eve she commanded, "Eve, follow Molly. Fear not, I will be with you."

After a few moments, the mirror held an image. Eve could clearly see High Priestess Hera sitting as she had always done, in the high-backed seat of her Sanctuary. She was, however, bound by black, viscous fibres. The thick strands seemed to be strangling her, cutting off her life-force.

Eve shuddered and tried to shout to the High Priestess but nothing came out.

"Calm yourself, Hera is beyond us at the moment. All we can do is observe. We must go deeper to understand. Seeing is only part of what we can do with our water mirror." Carlia breathed slowly in and out as she decided what would be the best course of action. She paused, allowing Eve to absorb the image, to gain a sense of what may be binding The High Priestess to her internal prison.

With sudden, clear insight, Carlia relaxed. She was now confident that they had discovered what they had set out to find. "Eve, it is time to return to consciousness. We have found the answer to our quest."

At their return, Carlia looked carefully at the expectant faces gathered around the fire and spoke. "Hera has been tricked into accepting rogue magic into the Sanctuary and I fear that it may be dragon magic. It has encased her in a web of illusion - she does not know that she is trapped. She is caught in a time-loop showing her the past that she believes is the present. It is clear that this problem lies beyond our capabilities to correct. I believe that Mage Hermes has found a remedy that will release his sister from this web of enchantment. But, Eve, I urge you to make haste to the

Emperor's castle because time is fast running out for your High Priestess - the spell is killing her."

~

After a week of hard riding, they arrived at the castle gates where the party were rushed into the Emperor's great hall. Instead of The Emperor, they were greeted by Mage Hermes' bent form.

"My dear friends," muttered Hermes, squinting his tired eyes as though the sun was too bright. "I, I am so happy to see you."

None of the group expected to see the Tarot Empire's Magician as aged and sickly as he now appeared. Their shocked looks caused him to comment: "I know, I know, you see me as an old man - I even feel old." His voice caught in his throat and he coughed as he directed The Hierophant, Follin and Eve to walk with him to the High Priestess' Sanctuary.

At the Sanctuary entrance stood The Empress, her grim expression enhanced by the gloom within. The Angel Temperance and the Star Lady were also there, silent, waiting to escort the group inside.

The Empress's voice was strained as she spoke. Her face flushed and her usually smart dress was crumpled as though she had been sleeping in it.

"The Wildlanders have used this opportunity to increase their attacks on our Empire," she said, there was an edge to her voice that neither Follin nor Eve had heard before. "The Emperor has had to rush to the Wands Kingdom to lend his support and has called upon the other Kingdoms to reinforce their brethren. All is not fairing well on that front nor in the Sanctuary itself. If it wasn't for Molly and Eve, the Sanctuary would have collapsed and our Empire with it."

The Empress led them to the very heart of the Tarot Empire. The first thing that hit them was the shocking smell, the rank stench of death and decay. What Follin saw next shocked him even more. The work of Molly, the Water Elves and the Angels Temperance and the Star Lady, had brought the High Priestess out of her invisible prison. Sitting in her high backed chair was the High Priestess, firmly bound in her chair by thick, black threads. It reminded Follin of a cross between a caterpillar's cocoon and a spider's web. Mage Hermes stood silently beside his sister waiting for the newcomers to take the vision in.

"We discovered that the Wildlander mages have used ancient magic to bind her mind and encase her body rendering her invisible to even the most critical examination. As you can see, Hera sits oblivious to our presence. She is powerless, believing that she tends the Sanctuary just as she has done each day." Hermes sighed and looked around at the sound of Eve sobbing.

"What can we do?" she cried.

Without speaking Mage Hermes reached into his robe and pulled out what appeared to be a seedpod.

"What is that?" asked Follin as Sox edged past Molly to sniff at the object in Hermes' hand.

At this display of interest, the Magician brightened. "That pod contains an incredible little creature I discovered in my wanderings. I never thought I would ever have need of it. Fetching it from the planet where it lives has cost me dearly, yet, if it frees my sister, then the cost will be worth it."

As he spoke the Magician bent down and attached the small, white seed-like pod to the edge of the web that surrounded the High Priestess. Upon the clicking of his fingers, the pod opened and out crawled a creature that looked like a caterpillar. It was surrounded by a dazzling aura which made Hera's webbed prison reflect the many colours of the rainbow. Molly and Sox leaned forward to watch as the creature immediately set to devouring the black strands that held Hera prisoner, just as a caterpillar would devour a cabbage leaf.

"That's amazing," whispered Eve, drying her tears on her sleeve to watch her mentor slowly awaken.

Hermes smiled, it was his first for what felt like a very long time.

"Yes, I do think this just might work," he released a long sigh of relief.

Eve pulled Follin to a bench beside the Sanctuary pool. They sat together to watch the caterpillar-like creature perform its task. Molly sat on Eve's lap studying the magical forms of Hera's enchantment and that of the creature freeing her.

"I can see Hera's feet now, but they are so pale, almost bloodless," whispered Eve.

"If Hera comes out of this relatively unscathed then we will all celebrate as we did at the Quest of Life," grunted The Hierophant.

The Empress and the two Angels watched the little creature, speaking softly to each other so as not to disturb the silent release of the Empire's most important Archetype.

Now that the excitement was over, Follin studied his aged mentor for a moment before walking up to him. "Mage Hermes? Earlier you said that going back to collect the caterpillar cost you dearly. Can you tell me what that means?"

"Certainly, that is part of the reason I've brought you and Eve along to witness this creature do its work." Hermes sat on the bench seat next to his apprentices overlooking the pool and nodded towards its slime-covered water. "This pool of water is a doorway to other worlds. We arrived here from our own planet via this portal you know." The fatigue and weariness in the Mage's voice had started to disappear but Follin could see that his mentor was exhausted.

"My many journeys to the other worlds had cost me my youth. In retrieving this creature my middle years have vanished as well." Hermes dragged his fingers through his greying beard. "When you saw me on your first journey through the Tarot I was in my middle years in terms of my power. Tonight you see me as an old man nearing the end of his days."

"What took your middle years from you?" asked Follin, concerned yet curious to learn as much as he could before Mage Hermes suddenly fell asleep - or worse.

"Power took it. That is the price for my many sojourns to other worlds to find the magic that would free my sister." Hermes gazed at the caterpillar slowly chewing through strand after strand of black energy. "I have undertaken countless trips into these worlds, crossing into unimaginably beautiful dimensions. But these days each trip demands more of my life-force than I can afford to lose. This last trip to bring back that creature has been the worst. I don't mind telling you that the journey nearly killed me."

"What does it take to travel across dimensions to these other places that make it so dangerous?" Eve asked.

"Power, you need to have enormous power to withstand the drain of energy that each trip demands of you. To collect that creature I had to cross in my physical form. One must be in physical form to return with a physical substance. I can travel in my astral body without cost, but in my physical body, that is altogether different."

"Does that mean The Charioteer can travel too?" Follin asked as he stared at the pond. Already some of the scum on the surface had begun to disappear.

"Yes," replied the Mage. "Sir Darwyn has made several such sojourns beyond this plane. But each has cost him just as dearly as it has others. In the early days, he was far more powerful than what you see now. These days he must use his Chariot, it protects him, to a degree."

"Does that mean these other worlds are dangerous?"

"Crossing dimensions in the physical body is an enlivening experience, a seduction that tantalises the senses beyond reason - but it is wickedly harmful to the physical body. The traveller loses essential life force with each journey."

"So why do it if it will kill you?" asked an inquisitive Eve turning to look away from the busy caterpillar.

"Mages have a burning desire to understand the world and beyond. These dimensions connect and unite with each other, they are like a maze, a network of energies. My teacher, The Emperor's previous Magician, Mage Willowtree, left this life to become a tree because his journeys beyond this planet were killing him. Rather than die a slow, debilitating death he transformed into a willow tree.

"When I took on the role of Magician to The Emperor, I tried to understand everything in the universe. I researched the many and varied forms of magic, and, to blow my own trumpet, I am the master of masters, the best mage the Empire has ever known." He paused to smile as he reflected on his many adventures. "This crisis, however, was completely unforeseeable and I am fearful of what the entrapment has done to Hera. If she remains unwell or deteriorates then so will I. We are linked so tightly that what happens to one happens to the other."

~

Follin's Meditation - Five of Cups

That night Follin dreamed, in his dream he saw the pictures of the Cups Kingdom and paused to examine the Five of Cups. It showed a despondent wanderer, three overturned cups lay on the ground at his feet while two upright ones stood beside him. Perhaps, thought Follin, he was dissatisfied with how his life had turned out and wished to set out on a new adventure?

Entering the image Follin called to the man as he strode over to greet him. "Kind sir, would you please tell me where you are going?"

The man looked up sharply, shocked to find someone standing beside him. "Hello, sir. Well, for your information I am about to embark on a journey, as you can see."

"I thought so, but these cups on the ground are spilled and those two are upright, can you please explain what this means?"

"You certainly are an observant lad," the man replied, a wan smile beginning to form on his lips to dispel his frown. "I have lived and worked in this city all my life, worked long and hard to build a very successful business. Recently a newcomer arrived who has turned the city leaders and my craft guild against me. I've been sitting here trying to drink my problems away, that is what those two empty cups show. But in my frustration and anger, I kicked the remaining three cups over spilling the last of my expensive wine. I'm frustrated at the rude barbarian who stole my livelihood, the city bureaucrats who deliberately suppressed my sales and I am angry at myself for spilling my wine!" The man stopped talking realising that he was becoming agitated again.

"I understand that you would be mightily frustrated at the rulers of the city and for spilling your expensive wine," added Follin.

Without looking at Follin the man continued, caught up in telling his sad story. "To be honest with you, I've handed the keys to my shop to my business partner and just walked out the door. All I have to my name are these clothes I am wearing and my jewellery tools in the pockets of my cloak. I've decided to try my luck in the city across the river. The citizens there are not as wealthy but they are known for their kindness and polite manners, unlike here. It seems that wealth and position breed greed and self-interest and I am powerless against that."

The man pointed to the bridge leading to a city on the other side of the river. "There is my destination. I have a cousin who lives there, he offered me a room so that I may continue to practice my craft."

"That isn't so far away, may I walk with you for a while?" Follin was curious to find out how the jeweller would fare in this new city.

"Of course, I don't own the roads! Oh, I'm sorry for being so rude, please understand that I'm not a good walking companion today. After all my years of hard work, I have nothing to show for it. My cousin has four children and is not wealthy by any stretch of the imagination. I will arrive empty-handed, seeking handouts from others. To lose my independence is something I have dreaded all my life. I'll have to start all over again, establish my name and my network of merchants to sell my products. It's all uphill… so damn depressing…" the man grew silent as the two started on the path leading to the bridge in the distance.

"Sir, you have years of experience and you have a place to stay. You have a friend in your cousin and his children to brighten your day. I think if you could keep your chin up and whistle while you work…" Follin knew how many a craftsman liked to sing as they worked, and many whistled, as he did when he was happy.

The man lifted his head and looked at Follin carefully. "Do you think so? I love to sing when I am working, do you sing?"

"I'm not much of a singer, but if you set a tune I'll whistle along with you." Follin let out a soft laugh of happiness when the man's stride lengthened and his voice lifted into song. It was a song Follin had heard many a time in the kingdoms and he whistled in accompaniment. Together they made their way across the bridge, their heads held high as they strode purposefully towards the man's new city.

Chapter 6 – Six of Cups

Family, security and safety, nostalgia.

Eve did not hesitate when asked by The Empress and the two Angels, The Star Lady and Temperance, to stay for a short while to help re-establish the integrity of the Empire's Sanctuary. She felt both delighted and honoured. At the moment she said 'yes' the atmosphere within the Sanctuary changed, vibrating with an intensity and urgency she hadn't experienced before. Why was the Sanctuary healing with such speed even though the High Priestess was in recovery and basically unavailable?

Eve inquired of The Empress, but she just smiled. When she asked the Angels Temperance and the Star Lady, they too smiled but offered no answer to enlighten her.

Follin visited her every day with Sox to marvel at this sudden blossoming of new growth and the almost ecstatic energy that now flowed through the Sanctuary glades. Molly was also aware of the changes but she too refused to explain why this was happening.

Mage Hermes' caterpillar had released Hera from the Wildlander mage's enchantment, however, she had no memory of the events that led to her imprisonment. As far as she knew everything was fine in the Sanctuary and there was no crisis.

The Empress patiently explained what had happened. She had shown Hera the uprooted trees, the dead birds and the patches of muck that remained on the surface of the pond. Hera was shocked when she saw the evidence of such devastation but was unable to process it. What did impact on her was the fact that she had failed to protect the Sanctuary and thus had placed the Tarot Empire at risk of annihilation.

Eve couldn't help notice how much Hera had aged during her entrapment. Not only was Hera noticeably older but her power was clearly diminished. As she could no longer protect the Sanctuary alone, the three female Archetypes agreed that they would remain by her side.

One morning The Empress called Eve to join them. "Eve, although your presence has accelerated the Sanctuary's healing, we have decided that you must return to your home in the Cups Kingdom. There is something special for you to do there, an initiation into something wilder and older than time itself."

"But, but you need me here," stammered Eve feeling lost and confused. She felt rejected. Perhaps she had failed them? "Look at how the Sanctuary has blossomed, it's thriving. It likes me, I can sense it." She looked apologetically at Hera but had to turn away when she saw how her words had stung her mentor.

The Empress saw it too. "Darling, Eve, we can clearly see how everything flourishes wherever you go," she said gently. "Hera's presence was very much the same when she became the guardian of the Sanctuary." Her voice softened further as she turned to Hera. "Hera, please do not be upset. The forces that imprisoned you have delivered a wound. The wounded keeper of the Sanctuary must one day step aside for youthful vigour, it is the way."

When Hera failed to reply, the Star Lady took up the conversation. "Hera, my love, when you are released from your guardianship you will be free to undertake the next stage of your journey. It is not the end, it is another beginning. I have visited the land of Shadows and have done so for many of your predecessors. I will prepare the way for you and your brother when your time comes - if that is your will."

Hera continued to sit in silence for some minutes before finally answering. "I am not jealous of you, Eve," she said calmly. "Never think that of me. I am grieving my failure to protect the sanctity of what I have called home for an eternity, I will miss it."

The Empress felt Hera's life-force fading even as she spoke. The task of engaging with Eve and the Archetypes at this early period of her recovery clearly debilitated her.

The once youthful beauty with the intense, vital presence that Follin and Eve had known, was now an aged crone. Her skin was wrinkled and cracked, her hair thin, without lustre or colour, her voice a mere whisper.

"Eve, your presence in the Sanctuary is highly regarded but you have other things to attend to right now." The Angel Temperance said firmly. "Go now to your home in the knowledge that the Sanctuary is safe in our hands and anticipates your return."

Eve looked at the four Archetypes and nodded in acquiesce.

The Angel took Eve's hand and kissed her forehead. "It is time for you to leave."

~

After several weeks ride and a short stay at the Water Elf village, the group finally arrived back at the City of Life.

On their second day back the Pages Kahmia and Jon dropped in after breakfast.

"Good day to you both," intoned Jon and Kahmia together. It was all too formal and Eve sensed that something was about to happen, perhaps it was what the Archetypes had hinted at.

In Kahmia's hand was a celebration goblet. She held it out towards Eve and invited her to accept it. Eve was taken aback when she saw a small, brightly-coloured fish swimming around inside. Follin stepped close to Eve and curiously peered into the goblet too.

"Eve, please accept this goblet. It affirms the special bond you have with the Cups Kingdom," Kahmia began. "Inside is a fish, it is a very special fish that must be carefully placed into your pond."

Giggling with excitement, Eve held tightly to the goblet as she stepped to the pond's edge. She didn't want to spill any water and lose the fish.

"Now dip the lip of the goblet into the pond water so that your fish can join the others," directed Kahmia.

There was a mischievous smile on Kahmia and Jon's faces as Eve carefully bent forward to dip the goblet into the pond.

Suddenly, before she had time to release the fish, a second fish leapt from the pond high into the air. With a flip of its tail, it dived into Eve's goblet. There were now two fish for her to place into the pond.

Follin gasped and Eve giggled in delight, but Kahmia and Jon were struck silent, shocked by what had just happened. They turned and looked at each other, their mouths opened and shut as they tried to speak. The Pages suddenly broke into laughter and began to dance. As though an enormous burden had been lifted from their shoulders the two Pages stepped forward and hugged the confused Mystic Isle couple.

"Congratulations to you both, you are soon to be the proud parents of twins!" Kahmia squealed in delight.

Over the coming weeks, visitors came from everywhere, dropping in to offer their help be it to cook their meals, babysit the twins when they arrived, tend their gardens or to do their laundry. Follin was overwhelmed and had to call upon Sir Rohan and Jon for help.

"Son, our people are caring and kind, but they'll smother you with their generosity if you let them. I hate to admit it but in many ways, this is a form of soliciting something from you in return. If there is one thing for you to master in our Kingdom it is to set boundaries and be prepared to say 'No'," offered the Cups Knight with a wink. "Our people love to give but they will always expect something back from you. Think of guilt as a trading platform, whoever arouses the guilt of another, wins. The Swords call it leverage, or in less polite terms, emotional blackmail. We all do it in one form or another."

~

Follin and their friends were in the habit of meeting at the beach after breakfast each morning to train in swordsmanship. The Knights Sir Rohan and Sir Darwyn excelled in all manner of weapons but not Page Jon. Jon was therefore a good partner for Follin. On their first morning, Sir Rohan arrived with a pair of nicely crafted wooden swords for the boys to use in their training.

"Follin, as you can see, Jon's sword is not one of Master Pew's. It won't stand up to the amount of training the two of you need. I can see by its enchanted weavings that your sword is designed to cut lesser quality blades in two. Although Jon's sword was made by a very good Bladesmaster many aeons ago, it won't last long against one crafted by a Blademaster's elemental as yours is." Sir Rohan handed each a hardwood sword that was the same balance and weight as their steel blades.

Follin wasn't so impressed. "Sir Rohan, that's rather... lame, isn't it? I mean, no one trains with toy swords in the Pentacles or Swords Kingdoms."

Sir Darwyn snorted as he tried not to laugh but it only caused Sir Rohan's manner to suddenly turn sour. The Cups Knight turned on Follin with a snarl. "These may be made of wood but they will serve for your training purposes, boy!"

Follin's head snapped around as he saw Sir Rohan's handsome face transform into a frightening mask of anger. He took a step backwards as Sir Rohan savagely threw a training sword at Sir Darwyn.

Lifting his own wooden sword high above his head Sir Rohan yelled a ferocious challenge. "And you, Darwyn! How dare you laugh at me!" His voice belied his normally gentle nature. "You over-sized cross between a swamp wraith and a rusted wagon wheel! Are you prepared to face a real warrior? The Master of the Dolphin Clan? An adept of the Merrow inner circle?"

The ferocity of his challenge had a dramatic effect on the bystanders who had gathered to watch their hero's usual morning training routine. Follin and Jon instinctively took several nervous steps backwards in fear. The look in Sir Rohan's eyes was terrifying. Follin always thought Sir Rohan was a bit of a fop, someone who just wore his sword for show. Surely the warrior of legend, Sir Darwyn, would kill Sir Rohan for his insults?

Sir Darwyn's face suddenly flushed bright red. It then turned purple to finally darken in anger.

"You braggartly son of a sea-weed infested pirate! I shall take great pleasure in sending your toy sword back to the forest whence it came, and your bloodied body shall make a fine breakfast for those precious dolphins of yours!"

With a rush he charged the Knight, swinging lustily at Sir Rohan's head, torso and legs. Each of Sir Darwyn's blows was met with a defensive stroke followed by a reflexive lunge that caused the Charioteer to pirouette, duck and weave defensively - sometimes with extreme difficulty. Twice Sir Rohan tapped the Charioteer on the arm and once on his leg.

There now gathered a group of onlookers six deep surrounding the combatants. They were completely transfixed by the ferocity of the two warriors. The fight was a mighty display of aggressive swordsmanship, balance and skill. Their two students of the sword pulled everyone back further to give the fighters more space as sword smashed against sword with such might that it sounded light cracks of thunder.

As the contest continued the audience were soon mesmerised by the skill of the two swordsmen. Cheers went up when a particularly savage thrust was met by an equally vicious parry. This was followed by a backhanded return jab at the face or body which would bring another cheer and shouts of 'bravo!'.

The spectators roared with amazement when Sir Rohan suddenly blurred into a whirlpool of motion. With a twisting leap, he was a water sprite. Another turn of speed and he had become a spinning tornado of swinging sword and dancing feet, which just as quickly morphed into a series of savage thrusts and bruising slashes.

Sir Rohan's attack reminded Follin of when he and Eve had watched a pair of dolphins hunting a school of small mullet just off the beach. The dolphins had twisted and turned just like Sir Rohan's swordplay. As he watched, Follin remembered that the Cups Knight was, after all, the Captain of the Dolphin Clan, his performance was no doubt based on the dolphin's moves.

Sir Darwyn's defences slowed as fatigue overtook him. The Charioteer, the champion of legend, finally leaned heavily on his wooden sword and waved his hand calling for a halt to their challenge.

It was the end of their display and the two swordsmen stood to attention and formally saluted each other. They then turned to salute the animated crowd. Sir Rohan stepped lightly across to his two students, a broad smile on his face that betrayed his joy at the looks of astonishment on Follin and Jon's faces.

"Well, Jon? Have you been practising your footwork?" He pulled his glove off to wipe at the perspiration on his brow. "And you, Follin? How quickly can you spin from a defensive parry to an offensive thrust? I do hope you lads had been paying attention."

Neither Follin nor Jon had an answer, the fight had shocked them into silence.

Once he had caught his breath, Sir Darwyn walked over and showed his students the damage to their wooden swords.

"Look, some bruising on the cutting edges but no splintering nor fractures. Nice work, Rohan, I think the lads should be quite happy with their toy swords now," he said as he waved to the crowd surging in to surround and congratulate their heroes.

Once again Sir Darwyn and Sir Rohan acknowledged the cheering crowd. This was a sight none had been witness to in the past. Swordplay was rarely celebrated in their kingdom but a display of skill such as this was sure to be spoken of for many years to come.

Follin finally smiled then a light laugh escaped his lips. "You, you both had this planned didn't you!" he laughed. "You had us so completely fooled, I thought someone was going to get killed." Sir Rohan and Sir Darwyn nodded with a light smile in acknowledgement.

Jon had remained quiet until Sir Darwyn asked him what he had learned by their display.

"Well," he said softly, "I think you, Sir Darwyn, deliberately went berserker at Rohan. I think that allowed Rohan to demonstrate how water-style swordplay can be used against an attack from a berserker. That's the Dolphin style, to evade, parry and then release a reflexive return thrust which would paralyse or kill their opponent." He suddenly smiled, he knew he was right.

Sir Rohan leaned across the space separating them and slapped Jon on the shoulder. "Little brother, you might be young but you've got an old head on your shoulders. Yes, that's what we had planned. However," Sir Rohan turned to look at Follin, "my anger was not premeditated. Sir Darwyn and I had planned this demonstration in advance but it was because you thought we were joking, Follin, that prompted me to release my frustrations out on my dear friend. And I must say, I did enjoy it. What about you, Darwyn? Do you think we've earned our lunch today?"

~

Follin enjoyed his weapon training routine so much so that he asked Ziggy if he would help him train with the bow as well. He was a reasonably competent archer but he wanted to continue to develop the skills he'd learned with the Swords Bowmen. Besides, he thought, who better to learn archery from than a Wood Elf?

It was decided that before breakfast each morning Follin, Ziggy and Sox would go to the beach for archery practice. The two would shoot one hundred arrows at their straw targets just as Follin had done with the Bowmen of the Swords Kingdom. Follin still had the muscular build of an archer though it was slowly being replaced with new muscles developed through his sword training. Follin particularly liked it when Eve ran her hands over his broad, muscled shoulders, saying that it made her tingle all over. It certainly made many of the Cups girls wish they could run their hands over him as well.

After his dawn training, Follin would have breakfast with Eve. More often than not one or more of their friends would drop in with something to eat from their gardens or food gifted by a neighbour. After breakfast had settled they would go down to the beach to begin their training in swordsmanship.

~

It was during this quiet period that Mage Hermes arrived from his convalescence at The Emperor's castle. He and The Hierophant had settled into the cottage next door and were provided with a maid to cook and clean the house while a scribe helped with Hermes' books and manuscripts. The Mage had hoped to finish writing his series of books on magic which he called, The Hermetica, but he well knew that time was running out and he might never finish his project.

Follin visited every afternoon to study the four magical tools with his mentor as well as to study the High Priestess' scrolls.

"And how are you coming along with those scrolls, Follin? Have you found the key to their wisdom yet?" Hermes would ask at each visit.

"It's hopeless. I've looked at the words and read the sentences but it means nothing to me. Even though I'm much better at reading, these scrolls seem to get harder and harder every time I unroll them," Follin would grunt in reply.

"Persevere and it will come to you," was the Mage's standard advice.

The Hierophant was also in the habit of asking about his progress with the scrolls and Follin's answer was always the same: "I'm doing well with my magic lessons but the scroll's wisdom still eludes me. I see the words but they just don't make sense."

It was one of those horrible humid days when there was not much to do but sit around and swelter in the heat. They'd all been to the beach to spent time in the cool ocean waters but by mid-afternoon, Follin and Eve decided to spend time meditating in the cool waters of their pond.

Follin arose from a vision, or perhaps he was hallucinating from the heat, or perhaps the pond fishes had spoken to him? He was certain that the High Priestess had said something, something to do with the secret of the scrolls. It involved Eve in some way.

Rather than disturb her, Follin waited for Eve to finish her meditation before speaking. It was still steamy and hot so they stayed in the pond sipping on a drink of fresh squeezed lime and grape-juice. Follin felt that this was a good time to ask Eve for help to unravel the meaning of his dream.

"I don't know what she meant but she kept saying, *'seek help from Eve regarding the scroll's wisdom'.*"

Eve looked at her husband for a moment before replying. "Hera is not well, Follin. Her energy is so low that it now takes The Empress, Temperance and the Star Lady all of their energy to keep the Sanctuary in balance. So why would she single you out now when she has so much to do?"

"Hera's special to me too you know, but… well, I don't know, but, what do you think Eve? What do you think Hera's message means? Can you help me with these scrolls, please?" Splashing the water with a dismissive flick of his hand he suddenly said, "You can have them if you want, they're useless to me."

Eve thought for a moment, this was the very first time Follin had asked her for advice on things of a magical nature. Normally it was the other way around. Besides, did she want to have the scrolls? What would she do with something that no-one could read?

"OK, we'll dry off then have a look at the scrolls together. Perhaps there's something in them that I can understand, though I doubt it. If you can't work them out what chance do I have?"

After they had dried off Follin brought the scrolls into the kitchen and placed them on the table in front of his wife.

"Here, look at this, it says on this first page, '*If you wish to know the secret of the scrolls ask and it shall be given.*' I've asked a million times, Eve, but it hasn't helped one little bit."

Eve unrolled more of the scroll. "These words look normal, Follin. I really don't understand why you couldn't read this. It's as easy as eating Mage Herme's mulberry pie."

This struck Follin as poppycock. He'd never been able to read beyond the first few lines. He now leaned across in front of his wife and looked. Sure enough, the words began to flow and he could understand every sentence.

"I don't believe it. How come I can read it now but not before?" he whispered.

As he spoke The Hierophant walked in to stand quietly watching them. He had brought with him a pot of coffee and a plate of honeyed oatmeal cookies – Eve's favourites.

"At last," he laughed when he saw that Follin had finally cracked the scroll's secret. "At last you've found the key to the scrolls, Follin. You took longer than every other apprentice before you to realise that the key was your partner, Eve."

"What? But if Eve is the key why did Hera give the scrolls to me?" cried Follin, confused as ever.

"The answer is in why we went to so much trouble to get you and Eve to meet during your Major Arcana journey. That took a lot of time and effort on everyone's behalf. Without the scrolls, you would not have been able to cross the rainbow arch and meet your true love." The Hierophant laughed when he saw the puzzled look on their faces.

"Of course there is more to this story than what I've just told you, but I'm sure that you get the picture." He turned to address Eve. "Eve, please take the scrolls as is your right. One day you will pass it on to the next Fool, a talisman that will help him find his true love, your successor."

~

Eve admitted to Page Kahmia that she had seen many a pregnant woman in her parent's healing room so didn't expect her confinement to be easy. She was right, morning sickness took its toll on her moods despite her initial joy at the prospect of becoming a mother. Even the smell of food in the morning caused Eve to race off to the bathroom. The Page decided that it would be best if she took over the running of her friend's household.

Eventually, things settled down, their friends and neighbours dropped by less frequently. When they did it was usually to deliver the gift of a delicious meal but only sometimes would they stay to share a cup of tea or coffee. Many an evening Follin, Jon and Sir Rohan would go to the beach with their visitors to give Eve and Kahmia some peace and quiet. On other occasions, they would visit The Hierophant and Mage Hermes in the cottage next door. At these times Mage Hermes was content to listen. He was still recovering and incapable of doing much more than enjoy the food, sunshine, fresh air and their friendship.

To Follin's amazement, he found that he was treated as a celebrity by the Cups girls. When they exercised in the mornings he would take off his shirt and go for a swim with Ziggy and Sox. Some of the younger Cups were now in the habit of joining them. They weren't there to learn archery or to exercise but to bask in Follin's growing status.

Most mornings there were many more females than males. The girls were always polite and interested in what Follin had to say. He liked how they complimented him on his tanned, muscled body and how good an archer and swordsman he was. They gushed over his cute Mystic Isle accent and they would often ask him to tell stories of his adventures through the Tarot Kingdoms. Some of the young ladies asked him to visit so they could show him their gardens and ponds.

Ziggy never said anything, he was quite detached from the Cups obsession with relationships. Sometimes Jon came down to practice with them. It was he who finally broached the subject and spoke of the problems that might occur if Follin agreed to visit the young ladies at their homes.

"These girls are after husbands, Follin, and the older women are looking for sons to dote on and spoil," said Jon trying tactfully to explain the reality of the situation without actually saying it.

"Jon, I heard one of them say I was 'adorable'. I think that might be a compliment?" Follin was sitting on the sand, Ziggy lay asleep between he and Jon.

Jon sighed. "Adorable? Really?" He realised that this was going to be harder than he expected. "Remember when Sir Rohan said you needed to set boundaries and learn to say 'no'?"

"Yes, I do. He said that was my main lesson here in the Cups Kingdom."

"Well, why don't you follow his advice?" Jon sat up and brushed dry sand off his back and sides. He too had begun to fill out and his tanned skin shone like golden honey. Follin looked around wondering why the ladies weren't bothering Jon.

"Why don't the ladies ask you back to their homes, Jon?" he asked.

"It's quite simple, I set boundaries. What do I say when they ask me to go out with them?"

Follin reflected for a moment. "You tell them that you're married and they would need to ask your wife first."

"Well?" said Jon looking at his friend.

"I see." Follin watched the waves as they gently surged up the beach towards their feet. It reminded him of the walks with his father to the local fishing villages on the coast and how his father liked to sit on the beach and watch the waves. "So that's what I should do too? Tell them to ask Eve?" he asked hopefully.

"No!" snapped Jon. "That's not what you should do. You can't just copy me, you've got to work out your own strategy." Again Jon sighed in resignation but softened as he remembered that Follin had no experience with these coy Cups girls. "I think we should work on your strategies together. In fact, let's think of ways to set boundaries and how to tell your flock of beauties to stop bothering you."

"But they aren't bothering me, they're really nice. They're friendly, and they're really kind." Follin studied the group of young girls sitting on the beach not too far away, watching the elf, the Mystic Islander and the Cups Page. He waved to them and their excited giggles floated back to him with the sounds of the waves.

"Look at them, Follin. They're like sharks waiting for Ziggy and me to leave you unprotected. Then they'll slyly wander over and gobble you up for breakfast." Jon laughed at himself, this was an apt description, he thought. "You've got to understand people's motives, what moves them, drives them to do the things they do. Us Cups are driven by our rampant emotions, we need to be needed. Some need to feel attractive and accepted; others need to be loved; some are lonely and need comfort and companionship. These girls who think you so adorable are driven by these invisible emotions. In setting your boundaries you must take this into account. Find what drives them and you will understand where to set your boundaries. Then you can say 'No' without hurting their feelings."

As Follin was digesting these words of wisdom, Ziggy yawned and sat up. He had heard every word of their conversation.

"Follin, what Jon said is quite true. People are simply animals, driven by very basic instincts. You call them feelings or emotions. Feelings are simple biological urges and instincts that enable them to continue their genetic line. Understand the specific needs of each person and you've completed your Cups lessons." Ziggy smiled at the two young men as he grabbed his shirt and pulled it on. He gathered his archery equipment up from the sand and called, "Come on, it's breakfast time, I'm hungry. You'll need to eat well this morning, I heard Sir Rohan say that he was going to work you both extra hard today. Something about breathwork, swimming and underwater fighting."

Jon looked at Ziggy and nodded. "Oh, I'd forgotten about the underwater fighting thing. I bet he wants to show us his secret Dolphin style. I think we're in for a big day, we'd better take a second breakfast with us on our way to training."

~

Follin's Meditation - Six of Cups

The image for Follin's meditation that night showed two children happily surrounded by six cups with bright, sunlit flowers sitting upright in them. The image appeared to represent the security provided by family and friends. It spoke of companionship and the joy of giving freely without expectation of something in return.

Another image now entered his meditation, that of the attractive young girls of the Three of Cups. At that thought, he saw the girls standing in the background of the Six of Cups image. They slowed their dancing to turn and watch him. At the moment they looked at Follin a flash of insight struck him: they had given him a gift, an egg, but no, it must have been two eggs. In his meditation he saw the two children, a tall boy and a slightly smaller girl, behaving like close friends, siblings perhaps? These must be his children of the future, the twins that the two fishes represented.

One of the dancing girls stopped her twirling and, walking seductively to him, placed her hand over Follin's navel. "Follin, your eggs are soon to hatch, when they do you will be blessed with the picture before you. The Six of Cups is a blessing, it comes from living as true to your principles as possible. Their lesson of this card is that if you make wise and appropriate decisions in life you will be rewarded. But for now, you need to work on your boundaries. Just remember, not every girl you meet has the pure motives of your wife."

Chapter 7 - Seven of Cups

Illusion, dreams, temptation, potential, choice.

It was obvious to everyone that High Priestess Hera and Mage Hermes were struggling to fulfil their teaching obligations. To assist them The Empress, Star Lady and Temperance took it upon themselves to mentor Eve, while The Hierophant and Sir Darwyn, the Charioteer did the same for Follin.

As things began to settle down Follin took to spending more time with Mage Hermes and The Hierophant in their cottage next door. Together they would sit outside under the leafy shade of an enormous mulberry tree eating cake and sipping coffee or tea. The Hierophant had become quite enamoured of the new beverage - coffee. Kahmia had taught him how to roast his beans in a frying pan on the stove and to then crush them with mortar and pestle. Finally, he would add boiling water to the powdered beans to complete his brew.

A local girl, Olivia, came by each day to help prepare the aged Archetype's meals and to do their cleaning and laundry. She was only a few years younger than Follin and had a bright, bubbly personality. Each time Follin visited she made a point to fuss over him as a bee would around a flower. Olivia was in love.

Mage Hermes and The Hierophant noticed what was happening as did others who dropped in to visit. The Pages Jon and Kahmia spoke to Follin on several occasions in the hope of getting him to see what was right before his eyes - the need for him to set his boundaries. To his credit, Follin tried to follow Jon's advice and find those elusive emotional drives and needs of this attractive young lady - but failed miserably.

After one particularly flirtatious interaction between the two, Jon broached the subject of Follin's dilemma. "One day Olivia is going to want more than a 'thank you', Follin. She's young, impressionable and attractive. When Eve discovers what's going on she'll be unimpressed - to say the least. I suggest you get cracking and learn about setting those boundaries we have spoken about," he advised one afternoon as the group sat in the shade of the Mage's mulberry tree.

"You, my good man, are setting yourself up for a fall, mark my words," offered Sir Rohan. "Men and women are programmed to flirt and fall in love, it's part of the 'birds and bees' thing. Believe me, I've had plenty of practice. I advise that you stop playing games with these pretty young Cups girls, you are giving them ideas that you cannot deliver on, Follin."

"But I'm not interested in Olivia, she's not even my type. I admit that I like the attention and she sure looks after me, but Eve is my one and only love. I don't know why everyone is telling me off for just being myself, it's not fair." Follin sulked, withdrawing behind the cup of tea in his hand.

"Follin, I told you before, set boundaries. Olivia comes from a large and respected family. If they think you've been leading her on they'll demand compensation," said Jon flicking cake crumbs into the pond to watch the fish leap up to gobble them down before they hit the water.

Sir Darwyn also offered advice. "If you dishonour a Cups person they will feel insulted and betrayed - and rightly so. That can lead their family and friends to seek revenge. Bad blood in the Cups Kingdom is not what you want. It could mean you end up parting with your property - or your life. That is if they don't convince you to divorce your wife and marry the girl first."

"I've seen Olivia look at you, Follin, she's got her eye on you. But I'm not going to waste any more of my precious breath trying to convince a bone-headed Mystic Islander to set boundaries designed to protect his marriage - especially if he won't listen. This will end in tears, my friend, a flood of tears," Mage Hermes said softly.

The Mage shakily moved his seat out of the scorching sun. "Right, everyone, time for Follin's lesson in magic." He turned to the Cups Page. "Jon, on your way out can you please go into my library and bring my four magician's tools? Oh, and keep them tightly wrapped, they don't like the salt air." He then insisted that everyone return at sunset for a special dinner.

The Mage had to push the cake, plates and empty cups to one side as he spread his magician's tools across the table. He would ask Olivia and her friends to clean the mess up in preparation for the evening's banquet.

"Follin, I think it's time I taught you the gift of the magician's cup. I hadn't needed to teach you of the coin or the dagger, you were quite capable of learning these yourself with the aid of your Pentacles and Swords teachers. But it seems that despite everyone's help here in the Cups Kingdom you just can't get your muddled head around this simple lesson of how to set boundaries."

Follin felt a surge of love for his teacher as he watched the old man fondle the cup in his hands with obvious familiarity and affection. Of the four magician's tools, the coin and dagger were the easiest to wield. Follin had spent much of his time over the years in studying their use. Because of his diligent practice in the Pentacles Kingdom, he found it much easier to apply himself to his tasks without too much effort. Because of his study in the Swords Kingdom, he could see through denial and an irrational or fanciful argument almost as easily as a Swords negotiator. One of his problems was that his blindness to this issue with the Cups girls clashed with his newfound Swords sensibilities. He could easily feel the conflict within but to access his emotional change point was impossible.

"Today we are going to work once more on what the Cup represents," Hermes said as he guided Follin to hold the magician's cup in his hands, close his eyes and listen.

"Mage Hermes, may I ask a question first?" Follin absently reached down to Sox sitting by his chair and scratched his ears. "I know the change point for the Cups, I saw it in the meditation I did with the Two of Cups. But I can't follow through with what I've learned."

"Follin," sighed his ever-patient mentor, "just take my magician's cup and follow my instructions."

Follin did as he was bid. He stopped talking, closed his eyes and grasped the cup in both hands.

"Now ease that grip of yours, you'll get a cramp," instructed the Mage. "I'm going to guide you to seek clarity of thought first, to see through the issues that confront you. I have a feeling that your head is all mixed up from trying too hard."

As the Mage began his narration Follin's mind formed a series of pictures that kept pace with the Mage's narration.

"I want you to apply what you have learned to the problem you have with the girls at the beach, and especially Olivia. Olivia is a gentle creature and deserves to be treated respectfully. I want you to contemplate what may be driving her behaviour, this will lead to understanding her change point. Then you can figure out how to set boundaries without hurting her."

Follin felt a moment of panic as he saw how his situation touched heavily upon his own needs. To someone who never had friends, who was bullied and alienated by his classmates, Olivia's friendship was extremely precious to him.

"Mage Hermes, I don't need to go into my deep unconscious to know this answer, or at least a part of it. Olivia represents something I never really had and that's friendship, someone who accepted me for who I am." Follin paused to think it through some more before continuing. "I believe that I keep her close to me because I fear rejection. I fear losing her validation that I am a good-enough person," he said finally.

"Yes, now tell me, what drives Olivia to pursue you so?"

"I am from the Mystic Isle and close friends to the Cups royal family and the Tarot Empire Archetypes. I think that Olivia is attracted to me because I am exotic, different to everyone else she knows, and that makes her a bit of a celebrity among her friends… And I think my paying so much attention validates her. She really does like me, and, oh dear, and I am leading her on by sort of flirting with her," mumbled Follin. "I was hoping that she was attracted to my lively personality and good looks, but I now see that there is more to it than that."

"Well done, young man. Now go deeper within, see if you can come up with a suitable set of boundaries so Olivia doesn't feel rejected."

Once again Follin felt himself easing deeper into his unconscious. When he came back he had the answer.

"Well?" asked the Mage, his smile made his face break into a mass of fine wrinkles. The mulberry tree's shade had moved, causing Follin to set his wicker chair in a sheltered position.

"I have to set firm boundaries for myself which means I need to heal myself first and that means continuing with my inner child meditations. I also have to demonstrate to Olivia that I appreciate what she is doing but only as a friend. I can't go into the bedrooms with her and laugh and joke like I've done. I can't let her touch me intimately as I've allowed. I can see that some of my behaviour would have been interpreted as that of a lover more so than as a friend. I need to stop that flirtatious style of communicating that

I've allowed myself to have with her." Follin's face was flushed red with embarrassment knowing that the trap he had fallen into was of his own making.

Mage Hermes nodded, his own eyes bright with amusement and satisfaction at Follin's answer.

"I can see how this became so puzzling to me. It was I who was projecting the need for acceptance and fear of rejection onto Olivia." Follin sat quietly thinking for a moment before replying. "If I reject Olivia outright I know that she will feel betrayed, it will harm her fragile Cups nature. She is so very much like me, I would feel rejected and betrayed if she told me to go away. But I have no choice but to be honest with her, I'm trapped by my own doing. As everyone said, there will be tears."

"You must now consider how to present this strategy to your wife as well."

Follin shifted in his seat nervously. "Eve is going to be angry with me. What if Olivia becomes jealous and does things? And, what if Eve rejects me?"

The Mage's voice was firm. "You haven't learned a blasted thing, have you? Isn't this the very source of your insecurities? This is something that you have just recognised within yourself. Name it!" he boomed.

With a wooden voice, Follin said, "I'm afraid of rejection, and I am afraid Eve will reject me. I'm afraid that by changing my behaviour all of the Cups girls will reject and abandon me too."

"Good, I think I have made my point. So your strategy is?" continued the Mage.

"I shall be honest with myself… and with everyone else. I need to make a firm decision for once in my miserable life," Follin said as if he was walking to his execution.

Mage Hermes merely grunted. "I give up. All that I've taught you and now you cringe when confronted with a simple problem like this. Sulking is not going to cut it, Eve will eat you alive if you go to her with that attitude." The Mage tried one more time. "Close your eyes and let's see if there is anything else inside that empty head of yours."

Follin did as he was bid and soon felt himself sliding into his deep unconscious. There appeared a screen which showed an image of himself speaking with Eve, explaining the situation to her. He watched as several different versions were run past him, a technique that he had learned from The Hierophant many years earlier.

"You have chosen your preferred scenario?" came the Mage's soothing voice.

"Yes," said Follin firmly.

"Now begin your water breathing and connect with Eve. When you have done that enter the scene and run through it several times. Make it as real as possible."

When Follin next opened his eyes he was in his own cottage. He was in the kitchen standing in front of Eve and Kahmia. The girls were baking bread ready for Mage Hermes banquet that evening. They stood open-mouthed, staring at him.

"Look who has dropped in, Eve, just the person we were talking about," remarked Kahmia as she wrestled with an obstinate lump of bread dough.

Eve looked at Follin with fire in her eyes and said caustically, "I hear that Olivia fancies you. I hope you haven't been leading that nice young girl on, Follin."

"I, I only now realised that I have been, but I am going to put it right," he said firmly, his jaw tight.

"Oh, I suppose you think that you can invite her here to help me with my house chores so that you can flirt with her some more?" Eve's eyes flashed fire again. Follin remembered to synchronise his breathing with her which caused her mood to settle a little.

"No, Eve, that's not it at all. I have made a firm decision not to play games with you, or Olivia, or with anyone. I will tell Olivia that I was rude and improper and that I am sorry. It is up to her, then, to decide if she will stay as Mage Hermes' serving girl." Looking directly into his wife's eyes he continued, "I have made my decision and I'm going to stick with it. I can't do any more than that." Follin stood tall and straight, his chest suddenly filled with power and his body radiated a strength that filled the room.

Eve stared at Follin and hesitated. There was a power, a confidence that she hadn't noticed in her husband before. "Well," she eventually said, her face shifting from a severe frown to one of acceptance. "Now that's out of the way will you please grab the baking tray out of the oven and put it over here to let the bread cool. We've only got a few more hours before we need to take everything across to Mage Hermes' house."

The dinner was a success. Mage Hermes and The Hierophant had deliberately arranged most of the food to be brought over by their visitors so that Eve and Kahmia wouldn't be overworked. They knew that Eve was easily run off her feet these days and that she could be quite emotional when stressed.

People came from everywhere to help and join in the fun. There were even some of the beach set - those who followed Follin in his archery and swordsmanship training. Throughout the evening sounds of laughter and song rang from the Mage's courtyard. One particularly popular song came up time and again to interrupt everyone's conversation.

We are the Merrow, the Merry Merrow are we!
We like the bogs, we like the rivers, but we much prefer the sea.
We like a kiss and we like a drink - especially when it's free.
Come party with the Merrow, the Merry Merrow are we!

The drunken singers would then lead a round-robin singing verse after verse of the Merry Merrow. It became so noisy that Kahmia had to take Eve and their friends inside where it was quieter.

"Come on girls, even hardened lasses like us can get fed up with the Cups anthem," Kahmia said as they sat at the kitchen table. They had to shift plates of food and mugs of wine and beer left scattered by the drunken revellers to make room for themselves.

By late evening Sir Rohan called for everyone to depart. The cottage and yards slowly cleared as friends and partners helped the more inebriated to get home safely, or to continue partying elsewhere.

"I've called you all here tonight," began Mage Hermes speaking to the small group that now formed his intimate circle, "to explain a few things. As everyone knows, Hera was imprisoned by the Wildlander magic. Somehow they tricked her and entrapped her mind in a memory loop. The elves suspect that it was a form of dragon magic which we understand is almost impossible to obtain, but again this is all speculation. The magic has injured her and through her, I too have been harmed. My travels to find a cure has also significantly injured us both and that has forced us into our twilight years."

"Mage Hermes?" asked Eve when The Mage had finished. "When will I be allowed to go back to the Sanctuary to help High Priestess Hera?"

"It is my understanding that you will be permitted once the twins are born. While they reside within your belly you cannot be exposed to the possibility of another Wildlander attack."

As the group listened to Hermes, the Angel Temperance appeared in the cottage doorway as a dazzling globe of light. It flooded the room with such brightness that everyone had to cover their eyes.

"Oh come on, Temperance," called The Hierophant pouring a mug of wine for their guest. "Turn it down and stop trying to impress the newcomers."

Some of the guests laughed but not Jon and Kahmia, they hadn't seen the Angel before and gaped open-mouthed at her dazzling beauty.

"I'm sorry, everyone, I simply don't get out too often these days. Can't I just enjoy myself once in a while?" The Angel Temperance giggled as she turned down her brilliant aura and reached for the proffered mug of wine. "Thank you, this is just what I need right now. I haven't had a drink since... my goodness,

Master Hierophant, when was the last time we got drunk together?"

Sir Darwyn started to laugh and Ziggy snorted wine out through his nose and started sneezing. The Hierophant simply poured her another drink, her first had already disappeared.

"It seems, Lady Angel, that right now is a very good time to get drunk. To answer your question, it was when Mage Willowtree decided to spend eternity as a tree, that was the last time we sat down together like this. If memory serves me correctly we didn't wake for three years."

"Didn't someone forget something?" laughed the Charioteer, sitting in the corner with Ziggy sharing stories of battle with a small group of rapt guests. "Isn't Lady Temperance the personification of 'temperance'? I would have thought you, of all our Archetypes, would be pouring this strong wine down the drain."

"Trust you to bring a wet blanket to the party, Darwyn. You always liked to point out my personal weaknesses," called Temperance from the other side of the room. "I tell you, this temperance thing has its drawbacks. I think that in a situation like this where we are staring at the Empire's total annihilation, getting drunk might be the best thing to do right now."

The night was one of temperance for most, but importantly the Angel's arrival helped everyone relax. As time wore on, the tension of what happened to the High Priestess and the Sanctuary started to ease. Sometimes knowledge isn't what people need, it is the reassurance that they aren't alone that counts most of all.

Follin pulled up a chair beside the aged Magician. "Mage Hermes, I wonder, is the change point for tonight in that chair over there? The chair with the radiant Angel in it?" He chuckled and patted his mentor on the shoulder.

"Well, my young friend, it certainly appears that way, doesn't it. Thank the gods and goddesses that Temperance has arrived. I was sure that I was boring the daylights out of everyone." He too smiled and sipped lightly as his own mug of wine.

But the Angel Temperance wasn't there to party. With a minimum of effort, she shifted her level of consciousness and cloned herself. One part entertained the party-goers and engaged as she would normally on an occasion such as this. The other part, her etheric clone, sought out Eve and tapped her on the shoulder.

"Eve, I am here on business. My charade out there has put everyone at ease and has given us the opportunity to do something of vital importance. Pan has asked me to escort you to his cave," Temperance announced in a whisper only Eve could hear.

Eve was sitting comfortably with the Pages and some of the helpers who had remained behind which included Olivia and a few of her friends.

"Lady Temperance, how am I supposed to do that? I'm entertaining."

"Simple, follow me." With a flick of her long blonde hair, Temperance guided Eve into her astral body and out of her chair. Eve was now a clone of herself, just like Temperance.

Eve could see herself, complete with her slightly rounded belly. She watched curiously at the expressions on her face as she continued in conversation with her guests. It was most surreal.

The Angel Temperance held tightly to Eve's hand as she led her into Pan's musty cave. It was only partially lit, most of the candles recessed into the walls were just a puddle of wax. She stopped when she saw two naked people, a man and a woman, loosely chained to Pan's throne. Surrounding them like playthings, lay a scattered mess of jewellery, gemstones, gold and silver ornaments, coins, apparel and exotic foods. None of this tempted Eve, she had heard Follin's story many times and felt quite prepared to ignore any temptation presented to her in Pan's bejewelled cave.

"My daughter," began Pan standing to greet her. "I am so pleased you could make it. I know that your day has been extremely busy and your health is still somewhat delicate." He bent and kissed Eve's hand inviting her to sit with him.

Eve noted that Pan was a little taller than the Angel. His face was well-formed, attractive yet not in a way that would bring admirers to his cave. He had a short brown beard and a pair of tiny horns adorned his head. What was most striking was his funny-shaped legs and feet which were those of a goat. As odd as he appeared she felt comforted by his warm presence.

"I understand that my friend, High Priestess Hera, has been injured and her health continues to deteriorate."

At the mention of her mentor, Eve nodded and tears welled up in her eyes. She wiped them with the only thing she had, her sleeve.

Pan politely handed Eve a cloth to wipe her tears. "I brought you here because I need to know if you are the right person to take Hera's place when it is time for her to relinquish her role as warden of the Tarot Empire Sanctuary." Pan looked into Eve's eyes as he spoke - observing, calculating.

Eve knew that he could see right through her, she could feel his mind dwelling gently inside her head. "I've done my best to attend to my lessons. I have the scrolls that Follin has carried with him throughout his journeys and I have properly assisted the High Priestess at every opportunity."

"I do not doubt the sincerity of your intent, my daughter. However, I need to be certain that you have the strength of character to take her place." Pan nodded at Temperance who spoke to Eve.

"Eve, Hera was a particularly willful child," the Angel explained. "Hera and Hermes were born on Runda Isle, they are endowed with elemental, human and Tarot blood. They were misfits right from the start. They fought and argued with each other and everyone else on the island. They were quite unpleasant to have around, I know because I helped train them."

"I remember someone telling me that Hera was a rebellious adolescent," offered Eve.

"Yes," said Temperance, "that she certainly was, but it also hardened her spirit. Of every possible candidate, Hera stood head and shoulders above them all. Her strength of character and personal courage marked her as the one we were looking for."

Pan spoke next. "Eve, do you have those same qualities? Can you uphold the virtues of temperance, charity, diligence, patience, kindness and humility? And can you rise above the sins of pride, greed, lust, envy, gluttony, wrath and laziness?"

Eve took her time to reply. "I've had a tough childhood, no one fed me with a silver spoon. I know how to manage hardship and when to wield a firm or soft hand when I need to. I believe I may be considered a suitable applicant for the position of High Priestess to the Tarot Empire."

"My daughter, Eve, I have a test for you but I must warn you that it will be painful. It may cause you to fling yourself to the ground in grief. Are you prepared for this?" Pan said softly.

"Eve, before you answer, please consider that Follin was sorely tempted and yet he passed my test. Your path is different and therefore your test will be quite different to Follin's - this test may break you," whispered the Angel putting her hand lightly on Eve's shoulder.

Eve's eyes widened but she set her shoulders straight and answered clearly.

"I have fought to survive when things were plunged into darkness in my homeland. I've been shattered by grief and loss, and yet I'm still here. So yes, I am ready."

Without warning, there appeared an apparition of herself nursing two babies outside her Cups cottage. She saw how beautiful the babies were, twins, a boy and a girl. Her heart filled with such love that she thought it would burst. She couldn't help but announce aloud, "Oh, how beautiful they are!" Her face glowed as she unconsciously rubbed her slightly swollen belly.

"Is this what you want?" asked Pan in his soft voice.

"Yes, oh, yes, it most certainly is!" Eve exclaimed honestly, totally immersed in the image.

"It is beautiful, I agree. Such love, such fulfilment and happiness...but look, there, coming towards you... it is Follin, and someone else..." Pan forced himself to remain silent as tears began to drip down his cheeks. He too wiped at his face with his sleeve just as Eve had done earlier.

The image showed Follin forcefully pulling the twins from the grasp of his screaming wife. He succeeded after a struggle and handed them to the woman standing, leering at Eve. The woman was of similar beauty and features to herself. One of the pretty Cups girls had finally won her husband, it appeared, and now she had won her babies.

"NO!" screamed Eve in despair. "NO! You can't do that, Follin! These are our children, ours, not hers!"

"Yet, if you become High Priestess, you may need to give your children to another woman to raise." Pan leaned forward to whisper softly into Eve's ear. "Are you prepared to sacrifice motherhood to become High Priestess? Have you the will, the dedication and courage to sacrifice everything you love to protect the Tarot Empire?"

Temperance was silently sobbing as she leaned against the god's throne. Her tears fell to the floor to land beside the man and woman at Pan's feet. The two creatures were in a state of sheer ecstasy, giggling maniacally as they revelled in Eve's painful trial.

"NO! NO! NO! I won't give up my children! Anything! Anything but my babies. Not my babies! You can't do this to me! YOU CAN'T DO THAT!" cried Eve wreathing in her chair as though wrestling with an invisible demon.

"The Tarot Empire requires the total abdication of all you love in this world. If you cannot promise that degree of selfless service then the Empire cannot trust you to put its needs above and beyond your own." Pan's face was hidden in his hands, yet his voice remained steadfast, unyielding. He allowed Eve to sob until she was no longer in the clutches of the apparition - for that was all it was, an illusion.

Eve now opened her eyes to see the two naked forms pointing at her and laughing hysterically. Then, as though awakening from a nightmare, she faced Pan.

"You hurt me, you deliberately hurt me." Eve stared with abject hatred at the god. "You swine!" She then buried her face in her hands as her body was racked by great heaving sobs.

"But," she cried, "But I know that it was just an illusion and I know that I am prepared to sacrifice everything for my Empire. I will willingly hand my children to another to repay the beautiful people who have supported and believed in me. You can do whatever you wish to me, but you won't break me." Eve suddenly stood and, forcing herself into silence, started to walk out of the cave. Her chest thrust forward in defiance, tears flowed freely down her face, but not another sob escaped her lips.

"Eve?" called Temperance softly as she raced after her. "Eve, stop, please."

Eve paused to face the Angel. "Step aside because I am done with this place!" Her voice sounded like the cracking detonation of a lightning bolt.

"I believe that Pan has something for you, a gift that you have earned this day," the Angel said smiling through her own tears. She held out her hand for Eve to take.

Eve started to cry once more. The pain in her heart was raw, she knew that she wouldn't survive another test.

"What does he want now! Hasn't he hurt me enough?" she snapped.

Pan stepped away from his throne to stand before her.

"Eve," he said softly, his tear-streaked face showed the depth of how terrible he felt for what he had put the young woman through. "I warned you that your test would be painful, the most painful anyone could ever experience. You passed with flying colours, just as we expected. Everyone I consulted agreed that you had within you a strength that even Hera lacked when she replaced her predecessor. Please accept the gift I now have for you." He paused and waited for Eve's response.

"I'm sorry," said Eve, her face dropped as she spoke. "I swore at you, you didn't deserve that. But you hurt me, you hurt me so much."

Pan extended his hand and lifted her chin. "Please, Eve, look at me."

As she grasped Pan's hand Eve found herself in a beautiful garden, very similar to the Sanctuary. Her heart filled with a warmth of love that threatened to overwhelm her. She saw that her mother and father, her little sister and grandparents were there with her. As she embraced her family she heard laughter. It was the delightful, giggling laughter of children. In her mother's arms, she now saw a little girl.

"Eve, may I introduce you to your daughter? Her name is Fiana, it means, 'warrior huntress'," said her mother, smiling with pride.

As she embraced her daughter she heard her father speak.

"Eve and I have the honour of introducing you to your son, his name is Aidan, it means, 'little fiery one'."

Eve felt embraced by the warmth of her family's love as she hugged her two children against her breast. Before the experience overwhelmed her completely Eve heard Pan's voice clearly in her mind.

"Eve, as High Priestess you will sacrifice part of your motherhood, for your task is demanding, but the fantasy of your trial will never come to pass - you have my word on that." As Pan's voice faded Eve found herself back in Mage Hermes cottage. She heard the sounds of people moving around cleaning up plates and mugs. There was a soft murmur of voices from outside where the men were seated around the fish pond smoking their pipes and drinking port from tiny clay mugs.

Beside her was the Angel Temperance, smiling.

"I, did I, were they truly my babies?" she asked the Angel.

"Yes, you did, and yes, they are. Now it's time for you to go to sleep, you've had one hell of a night." Temperance giggled at her little joke as she reached down to help Eve out of her chair. "It is late, let me put you to bed."

~

Follin's Meditation - Seven of Cups

Follin struggled to fall asleep that night. Beside him, Eve tossed and turned as well. When he synchronised his breathing with hers, he sensed that she had passed her trial with Pan. Although he saw no details nor recognised the actual images he knew that it had traumatised her, yet she was wildly excited about something else.

Try as he may, Follin could not fall asleep. In the end, he gave up and went to the lounge room. Sox crept quietly after him and the two curled up on the sofa together.

"Come on, Sox, let's go into the picture of the Seven of Cups, this might be what my spirit wants. Seven cups with seven choices, dreams and illusions, a fantastic display of nice things to tempt me."

Follin entered a light trance and saw Sox waiting for him on a mountainside. 'This must be the Hindamar Mountains,' thought Follin as Sox led him to Pan's cave.

Pan met them at the entrance to the cave. "Follin, I've been expecting you, come inside, I have someone I wish to introduce to you," he announced.

Inside Follin saw the same naked man and woman sitting in chains on the floor, they ignored him. Surrounding them were plates of food, delicacies Follin could only dream of. He turned to Pan and waited for the god to speak.

"Follin, I am sorry for Eve's restlessness, her test was traumatic. We knew she would pass but she needs you now more than ever. Be attentive to her needs and she will heal in time. What you also sensed was something special, she met your son

and daughter. I am sure that she will tell you all about it in the morning." Pan paused as he led Follin and Sox deeper into his cave until they faced a large image painted on the cave wall.

"Here is your lesson, the Seven of Cups. I wonder, would you care to interpret it for me?" Pan lifted one eyebrow and smiled, a charming, pleasant smile.

Follin responded in kind. "Why certainly, my Lord." Follin felt quite comfortable in the god's company. He studied the image and stepped into it as he had done many a time in his scrying meditations.

Follin spoke to the man in the image. "Kind sir, what is it that you are doing? I see you have many options, yet, why do you hesitate?"

The man looked at Follin and studied him for a moment. "Don't I know you?" he quizzed as he strained to recall this familiar face. "Perhaps I do perhaps I don't. However that may be, I see before me many options yet not a one satisfies me. Apparently, I must choose one, so I will take my time and weigh up each before making my final decision."

Follin nodded his head, this was a good plan, he thought.

"That cup covered with a cloth, I wonder what that represents?" Follin said out loud hoping to attract comment from Pan.

"That," answered Pan, "is the unknown, a gift that may require the chooser to draw upon his own powers to manifest."

The two stood quietly as they waited for the fellow to make up his mind.

"Kind Pan, I have decided," announced the young man still looking at the images on the wall. "I believe that I must first grow *as a spiritual being before I accept a gift as pure as the one sitting at the top. An unknown quality that draws upon the user's own power must be something of great value. These others are illusions of wealth, promises of power, fame and success, I care not for them."* The man turned to Pan and continued. *"If I may, I will return when I am ready. I can enjoy my dreams as much as I like while I sleep but reality is forever."*

He turned to Follin and bowed low. *"Sometimes one must recognise when one is confronted with a phantasm. The mystic does not build his life on illusions and fantasies. If I am to become what I seek then I must recognise the value in all things. Sometimes one must say 'No' even to the great god Pan when he offers his gifts."*

"A single moment of enlightenment is priceless," replied Pan bowing to the man. *"However, enlightenment is but a fleeting moment in the life of the mystic. What one sees today will always be viewed with different eyes the next. Sir, go with my blessing, you have passed your test. I look forward to the day you return to complete your challenge."* As the man disappeared Pan turned to Follin and asked, *"Follin, what is the lesson here? What have you learned tonight?"*

Follin bent to scratch Sox's head as he tossed the question over in his mind.

"It seems that this man is on the mystic's path and has undergone a test much like Eve and I experienced. He refrained from making a decision when he saw that he didn't have enough information to make the correct one. He also recognised that life presents many illusions that many of us believe are real. We all like to day-dream and think of what we would like to have, but the

reality is that what we want is not always what we need. I like that fellow, he reminds me of someone... who is he?"

"That was the answer I was seeking, Follin. As to who this mystic is, well, let me just say that you will meet him on your journeys soon enough." Pan took Follin back to the cave mouth and bent to tickle Sox under the chin. "It is now time for you to return to your bed. Sleep well my son, and keep to your mystic path, for that is the only thing that will save you in the coming challenges that face the Tarot Empire."

Chapter 8 – Eight of Cups

Tying off loose ends, embarking on a new adventure.

The following day Follin stepped into the Mage's cottage and walked over to where Olivia was preparing afternoon tea. There was no one home, Kahmia had taken Eve to the local hospital to assist in their healing clinic as she did most days; Mage Hermes and The Hierophant were with Sir Rohan in the local rehabilitation hospice; and the rest of his friends were busy elsewhere. It was the perfect moment for him to say what had to be said.

"Hello, Olivia, I need you to walk with me, I have to speak with you." Follin hurriedly brushed his sweating palms down his shirt front in an attempt to dry them.

The winsome young woman looked expectantly at Follin, a knowing smile swept across her face. "Of course, I would love to." Her lips parted slightly as her breathing became faster, she reached across the kitchen bench to hold Follin's hand.

Follin moved back and away from her grasp, then walked briskly to the door, Olivia followed just as quickly. He kept at the same pace until he reached a rock on the sand where he and his friends regularly placed their weapons when they did their training. Olivia finally caught up and sat next to Follin. With a suddenness that surprised him, she thrust her arm through his and pulled him tight into her bosom.

Fixing his stare on the ocean waves in front of them, Follin hesitated for a moment before speaking. "I'm, I'm sorry, Olivia, I've done wrong by you and I need to set it right."

"Oh my, I didn't expect this so soon, Follin, but you've just made me the happiest girl in the Kingdom," she gushed sweetly squeezing his arm and leaning forward to kiss him.

Follin pulled back and tried to remove his trapped arm from hers.

"No, no, you've got it wrong. I don't know how to say this without hurting you, but I know that I've been flirting with you, and that's wrong. I have to stop, we both have to stop. It's my fault, I should have known better but I didn't. I'm sorry, Olivia, I really like you but I've made… oh, this is so difficult. I can't give you the love that you want from me," Follin stammered moving his face aside in an attempt to avoid her urgent lips.

"Oh? But… you… you what!?" Olivia suddenly jerked her head back and emitted a stifled scream. Her sweet lips parted to erupt into a torrent of pain and outrage. "I thought you wanted me!

I thought you were going to leave that fat, nagging wife of yours for me! You tricked me, you lied, you cheated me!" Gasping to catch her breath, Olivia burst into tears. Then, releasing her grip on Follin's arm she buried her face in her hands.

"I told everyone you loved me and that, that, you were going to take me away from here. I, I thought you loved me because we did all those things lovers do. You all but said you loved me…" Hot tears smudged her rouged cheeks as wet mascara blackened her eyes. "I love you and I will love you forever, Follin. I'd rather die than have you abandon me," she sobbed into her hands.

"I'm sorry, Olivia, what can I do but say I'm sorry?" Follin tried to pull away as Olivia grabbed his shirt front and buried her face in his chest.

All of a sudden she lifted her face and screamed, "You scoundrel! You can go to hell!" Olivia brutally shoved Follin away and stood rubbing the tears from her face. Without looking at him she turned and ran along the beach, her figure eventually merged with the sea mist in the distance.

A sudden horrible thought struck Follin, *'What if this sets Olivia on a path of revenge just as Sir Darwyn had warned?'*

He tried to catch his breath as his panicked mind raced through a number of unpleasant scenarios. Would her family seek some sort of restitution? But then an even more horrific thought struck him: what if she went home and harmed herself, or worse?

'I need to go for a walk or visit my pond or something. I'll go mad if I don't stop these horrible images.' Follin shuddered as he breathed deeply into his navel to stifle the panic attack he felt rising in his chest, then slowly walked back to his cottage.

The next morning Olivia failed to show up at Mage Hermes' cottage, so Follin decided to speak with his mentor.

"Mage Hermes," began Follin awkwardly. "I spoke to Olivia yesterday, as you know. But, well, now I'm worried that she may have done something to herself."

The Mage looked at his apprentice and slowly nodded his head in response. He knew from his own experience that the young carry a dreadful burden on their shoulders when things get out of control.

"Olivia is being cared for at Rohan's rehabilitation hospice. She is in good hands but she is grieving her loss, a loss that comes with expectations that have turned into dusty illusions." He saw that Follin struggled to understand so explained further. "Olivia knew that she had little chance to turn you from Eve, and to her credit, she didn't try. She instead expected her charm to win you over, and I must say that she very nearly succeeded, even though you have yet to accept that fact."

"I didn't do anything, honestly, I didn't think of her like that. I just liked being around her and the other girls, I've…"

"Be that as it may, Follin, Olivia is in therapy. I believe that she has taken a liking to the care provided by the hospice too. If destiny works in her favour she will make a fine counsellor herself once her stay there is over."

Follin stared at his mentor, uncertain of how he should feel.

"She doesn't know it yet but with a little guidance from myself, Rohan and Eve, she will look at a career in healing. I have examined her astrology chart and can clearly see her healing potential. And yes, Eve has been helping her, but I asked that she not say anything until I had spoken with you."

~

Mage Hermes and The Hierophant enjoyed having visitors, often inviting them for coffee and cakes under the mulberry tree. The tree's thick canopy of branches spread wide enough to seat a dozen visitors. On rainy days the visitors could either sit outside under the tree or around the fireplace in the cottage's over-sized lounge room. It was here that many a conversation started and would sometimes run long into the night.

"We're not useless, Follin," explained the King of Cups on one of the Royal couple's rare evenings away from their water castle. "Don't forget, we have far more experience in magic than both you and Eve put together. We may not be on par with Hermes or Hera, but the Tarot Kingdom rulers know a thing or two."

"Yes, but," countered Follin, "what if the Wildlander mages are using something like black magic?"

Mage Hermes interrupted the conversation, as he had done a few times already. "Excuse me, Your Majesty. Follin, I've told you on countless occasions, magic has no allegiance to anyone – and there is no such thing as black, white, green or pink magic."

"I know but I'm just worried. I'm worried about what it could do to Eve and my children when they visit the Sanctuary." Follin's frown produced lines of tension that seemed to have etched themselves across his forehead.

The Queen of Cups offered her thoughts. "Follin, I know how much you worry for Eve and your future children, but The Empress reports that there is nothing to suggest the Wildlander's magic remains in the Sanctuary. They have kept Eve away just in case, but that's simply a precaution."

Follin pressed his temples with his hands. The closer the birth of his children the more time he spent worrying.

"I can't help it, I'm just worried. I seem to worry every spare minute I have these days," he sighed.

Sir Darwyn and Ziggy had been listening and decided that now was a good time to rescue their friend. The two escorted Follin across the back garden to sit beside the fish pond. There was a misty, light rain but the night was pleasantly warm.

Ziggy pulled some shredded tobacco from his leather pouch and, leaning over to protect this precious leaf from the weather, prepared his pipe. The Charioteer waited for Ziggy to hand him the pouch so he could fill his own. Almost as though deliberately ignoring his friends Follin watched the tiny raindrops form patterns on the pond surface next to him.

"Follin, remember how I said that I needed to visit my clan in the forests? I was wondering if you would like to join me on another adventure?" asked Ziggy drawing on his pipe. As soon as he knew the date that Eve would give birth to the twins he had started to plan his visit to his Wood Elf village. "Eve still has a few months before she delivers the twins, why not spend part of that time with my people?"

Follin absently rubbed at his face as the misty rain formed rivulets that tickled his skin.

"I'd better ask Eve, she might get upset. She's not been the same since she met Pan. She's become really moody and worried about losing the babies, but I'd love to go if she lets me." There was a faint flicker of a smile that sought to chase the frown from his face.

Sir Darwyn yawned, it was late. "We already did and she said 'yes'. Eve wants you to get out from under her feet. She told us to take you away and only bring you back when she is ready for the birthing. Phew, she was rather expressive too, I know what you mean about being moody."

Follin's eyes brightened and he smiled in delight. "She said I could go?"

"Yes, and now we can all get out of this rain and into bed. We'll prepare for the trip after training tomorrow. Page Jon will accompany us but only to the Water Elf village. He wants to spend time with his cousins there." When Ziggy had finished speaking he smiled too. It had been some years since he last spent quality time with his Wood Elf clan.

As one of the commanders of the Elf Rangers, he was responsible for patrolling alongside the Wands Fearless commando. When he returned home from his last patrol, Sir Darwyn asked if he would like to join him in protecting Follin and Eve on their sojourns through the Kingdoms of the Tarot Empire. The Archetype and Wood Elf decided to remain as the Mystic Islander's guardians throughout their time as apprentice magicians.

~

Eve knew that her meeting with Pan was a pivotal moment in her life yet it left her feeling vulnerable and nervous. Not only would she soon become a mother but she would also have to sacrifice some of the joys that motherhood brings.

"Kahmia, all I'm doing is sitting and waiting, but that makes me feel guilty. Hera needs me and I can't be there for her," she complained.

Kahmia had also dedicated her life to her people and what Eve was going through resonated with her.

"First things first, Eve. Right now I think you need to focus on preparing yourself for childbirth," she said trying to calm her friend. "Luckily for you, we have a special birthing ritual in the Water Castle."

"Sure, what is it?" Eve asked woodenly.

"Goodness gracious my girl," Kahmia said playfully, "every day that we go to the beach and swim I'll take you to the Water Castle. The midwives there will teach your twins how to breathe properly - before they are born. In fact," Kahmia put her fingers to her forehead to think, "I have a feeling the twins may even develop certain Cups characteristics, the nice ones of course."

So it began. Every day the two would practice the water breathing meditation with the midwives beneath the sea. It was during one meditation that Eve saw her children again.

"Kahmia! I saw them, my family and my children. Their smiles… oh so sweet! And the love was like an ocean current that went right through me," said Eve excitedly.

"I told you that water breathing was powerful."

Eve also had a question that had been troubling her for some time.

"Kahmia, I've always wondered, how did you know that I was pregnant the day you gave us the cup and the fish?"

"Well, you see, Cups people just know things. In fact, we knew about it the moment you conceived."

"Oh, how embarrassing," Eve giggled. "But the fish and pond thing, what was that all about?"

"Fish represent fertility in our Kingdom, and the pond is the unity of spirit and happiness. Every family has a pond, so, placing a fish in someone's pond is a ritual of fertility, happiness and success in life. It is usually passed down from the parents to their children when they wish to start a family of their own. In your case, Jon and I had that honour. It was pretty special wasn't it?"

"Yes, it was, and a huge surprise when you told us we were having twins," replied a much happier and contented Eve.

~

Ziggy left with Follin and Page Jon in the early morning. By evening they stopped at one of the taverns along the Pilgrim's Way. They were happy not to have to spend their first night under the stars on the cold, damp ground. Ziggy retired early to do his ritual meditations. This did not stop the exuberant Jon taking Follin downstairs for a plate of the tavern's delicious curried lentil pie and a mug of their famous brown ale.

"Good evening, Page Jon, have you brought a pilgrim to visit the healing shrines of our elf cousins? The pilgrim season hasn't started yet but the hot springs will be most welcome in this miserable weather," announced the rosy-cheeked tavern girl serving the two young men at their table.

"Nay, Miss Tumlin, not on this trip. My pilgrimage isn't for another few months yet. Besides, you may have noticed that I am not wearing my seashell talisman. No proper Cups pilgrim ventures forth without grabbing a shell from the beach as a gift for the keepers of the shrines." Jon lifted his eyes to the young serving girl and smiled, his charm wasn't lost on her.

"Well then, sir, what are you doing out in this damp weather?"

"This is just a trip to stretch our legs and say hello to our elf cousins," Jon said disarmingly as he reached across Follin's plate to grab his mug of ale. "You can expect to see me on my pilgrimage in a few months time. Perhaps Follin here will bring his wife and newborn babies."

As they set to eating their generous portions of pie, Follin politely asked, "Jon, is this a good time for you to tell me about Sir Rohan, and why he was banished from his the Cups Kingdom?"

Jon thought for a moment. "Yes, this is as good a time as any to tell you about my big brother's banishment. Rohan sometimes still speaks of it so it's not as though I'm speaking out of turn. My brother, Rohan, is widely recognised as a chivalrous and brave warrior. He spent many years on our Empire's northern borders with the Wands' Fearless Commando, the Pentacles Mountaineers, and the Elf Rangers. There he learned about hardship and what it was like to be truly afraid in battle. Because of his experiences on the frontier, he decided to set up hospitals for the wounded and traumatised soldiers. Eventually, these included refuges for displaced and homeless families forced out of their homes by the fighting.

"When he arrived home he was worshipped by our people. Not only was he now a warrior of repute, but he shared his generosity and kindness among the people of our Kingdom. He would regularly travel from village to village to help bring in the harvest; the building of seawalls for the safety of the fishing vessels and crews; making sure the country folk were fed and well cared for by their overlords, that sort of thing."

Follin finished his pie before asking Jon to pause his story while he went to the bar and brought back two foaming jugs of ale.

"Go on, Jon," encouraged Follin, warming to his story.

Accepting the mug of ale from Follin's outstretched hand, Jon continued. "In the City Of Life, Rohan set up refuges for pilgrims and travellers, the poor, the sick, the homeless and the destitute. My brother has a very kind heart, but it wasn't always like that. Rohan was a passionate young man and made a sacred oath to only marry one person, his soul-mate. Sadly, he had the terrible misfortune of falling in love with a married woman who happened to be happily married to a cloth merchant's son. Despite the woman's vows of marriage, my besotted brother wooed her mercilessly. This not only caused embarrassment to himself, but also to the woman he loved, her husband and family and the people of the city."

Follin nodded as he recalled how the Two of Cups was the key to understanding the Cups people. It was about seeking a balance between one's wild passions on the one hand and accepting the cold logic of the situation on the other. Sir Rohan himself had said that setting limits to one's emotions was the lesson of the Cups. Now the Knight's comment made sense to him.

Jon continued, oblivious to Follin's sudden insight. "I was lucky. When I was struck by Cupid's love-arrow, Kahmia was happy to marry me." He smiled, unconsciously twisting the ring on his finger. "Well, one day it all came to a head. After the woman had rejected him for the umpteenth time her husband and his family petitioned the King, asking him to step in and reprimand his son. Our father did so but it only caused Rohan to feel betrayed. He took to his room and wouldn't come out. Rohan started drinking heavily and quickly degenerated into a nasty, violent drunk.

"As you know, we use the water breathing meditation to release stress and other unpleasant emotions we are plagued with, but Rohan even stopped doing that. We are of the Royal Merrow, and Rohan, as head of the Dolphin Clan, well knew how to bring himself back to a balanced state of mind. Unfortunately, he refused to let go of his infatuation with the woman, and so he sought revenge for her rejection and humiliation.

"My brother could have gone to the Water Castle at the bottom of the sea to be with the King and Queen but he didn't. Instead, he tried to drink himself into oblivion. But when that didn't work he allowed his anger at what he believed to be an injustice, to dwell deep in his heart. His jealousy became a suppurating, abscessed wound. The King eventually took him aside and explained that a man of his position must exercise greater control of his emotions.

"'Son,' said the King, 'It hurts your mother and I to see you this way. We have rejoiced in your successes and know that your heart is kind. You were never cruel, as some people in positions of power can be. All we ask of you is that you leave this woman alone. You have shamed her and her family enough. Now you bring shame to yourself and our people.' The King then reminded Rohan of his duty to set an example as Cups Royalty, to set boundaries to his passion."

"What did your brother do?" Follin asked, entranced by Jon's story.

"Rohan sat through the conversation with our father without saying a word. He waited in silence until father gave up and left. It was then that Rohan decided to have his revenge on the woman who scorned him. His desire for vengeance blinded him to reason."

Follin's second ale sat untouched on the table. "I can't imagine Sir Rohan wanting to hurt anyone."

Jon smiled, but it was a smile that an adult would give an ignorant child. "Follin, Cups are passionate people. We are tossed about by the turbulent nature of our emotions. Rohan spread spiteful gossip of the woman and her husband. Nasty rumours of infidelity. They weren't true but they spread like wildfire. Our people love to gossip. We have a saying, *'If a honeybee is seen in the morning to announce the first day of spring, the entire Kingdom will lay claim to having seen it by lunchtime'*."

"Was your brother really that bitter and vengeful?"

"His pride was hurt, but it was more than that. A Royal Merrow of the Cups Kingdom lives and dies by their honour. Don't forget that Rohan had sworn a sacred oath that he would only marry his true love. Because he loved a married woman he was destined never to marry, ever. He would never have children and thus never provide an heir."

Follin stared at the barely touched ale in his hand. Unconsciously he lifted it to his lips as he listened with rapt attention.

Jon continued. "Our father had no choice, he banished Rohan from the City of Life for twenty years. During that time he lived with his Dolphin Clan, the Water Elves and then served with the commandos on the Wands northern borders. It was while serving in the military that he came to terms with his vengeful nature. Where he was a lust-filled youth at the time of his banishment, he returned to our people as an honourable and respectful man."

"Jon, did you say that Sir Rohan served with the Fearless Commando in the Wands Kingdom?" asked Follin.

"Yes, he served with them for many years helping to protect our northern borders. He saw firsthand the impact of the violence and savagery of war on the Tarot Empire. The displaced farmers and the decimated villages as well as the returned soldiers who had nowhere to go, wanderers broken in body and spirit. It was during his service with the commandos that he recognised the need for healing of those affected by the fighting." Jon took a mouthful of his ale before continuing.

"When he returned to the Cups Kingdom, Rohan set up hospitals and hospices everywhere. We have a wonderful affinity with the four Tarot Kingdoms, thanks to Rohan's work. He taught us how we might show respect for the sacrifices of our brothers and sisters of the Empire."

Jon looked at Follin and smiled brightly. It was a pleasant change from the serious nature of his story. "Did you know that the hospitals are different for each Kingdom? No? Well, here in the Cups Kingdom, we have special hospitals for the lonely and abandoned in love, like Rohan was. We call our specialist healers 'counsellors' or 'therapists' and our hospitals are sometimes called 'sanatoriums'. Our people get so maudlin that we decided to pass a law that all tavern keepers cut their wine and beer alcohol content to half strength. It helps us manage our drinking problem. We turn to drink as a means of coping with our self-indulgent and capricious feelings."

Jon chuckled before continuing. "The Swords have refuges for the delusional and anxious. The Pentacles can become despondent especially when rapid change is forced upon them, like when a new way of doing things arrives in the Empire. They struggle to keep pace with change."

"What about the Wands?" asked Follin, enjoying Jon's novel explanations.

"The Wands?" chuckled Jon. "What's not wrong with them? They have refuges set aside for those injured at their wild parties. There is not a single party that doesn't end up in a fight or a dare that puts someone in hospital. And if you think the Cups have a problem with drinking to excess then you should attend one of the crazy Wands' parties. To be honest, though, Sir Rohan was amazing. He set up a means to help those injured in mind, body and spirit. The Empire never had anything like that before."

The two sat silently in thought, their mugs of ale sitting barely touched in front of them. Finally, Follin spoke. "I like Sir Rohan, he is a real gentleman. That explains why, at his age, he has no wife or children... so I guess he has an Aries Moon?"

"Yes, plus Sun and Venus sit in Scorpio in his 7th house. He has a hot and passionate nature indeed. What is sad though, is that my brother will never father a child. Kahmia and I are responsible for the Royal Merrow line now."

"I wonder... Jon, if you don't mind me asking, how old are you?"

"How old do you think I am?"

Follin thought for a moment. "When I saw you for the first time I thought you were the same age as me, in your early twenties."

Jon laughed. "Double that and you're close. When we merged our blood with the Water Elves we also took on longevity. Our King and Queen don't have immortality, instead, they use the water breathing meditation exclusively. This gives them extra years of grace before they pass to the Shadowlands." Jon paused to sip once more at his mug of ale. "Those of us who practice water breathing beyond our childhood can sometimes sense the future. It gets stronger after we've undertaken the Quest of Life. Even though we live longer than those of the other Kingdoms, we are very mortal. In some ways, when we do pass over to the land of Shadows we'll feel an enormous release."

Follin shook his head in confusion. "But why would you feel relief?"

"We're almost too fragile and vulnerable to survive in this world." He paused for a moment to sip at his ale. "You will rarely see a Cup warrior, Rohan is an exception. Warfare terrifies us. Rohan is a master swordsman and although he fought with the Kingdoms of the Empire he said that he never killed anyone. He always said that with heartfelt relief I might add."

"I'm sensitive too, Jon, but I don't think I'll be relieved to die."

"Ask the elves why they hide in the forests, Follin. Ask Ziggy or Ardler or Carlia, they'll tell you what it's like." Jon's face hardened. "Remember the water breathing meditation you learned for the Quest of Life?" Follin nodded. "You must also remember the incredible joy you felt. Well, that meditation sensitises you to everything. We meditate in our pond and the ocean so that it buffers the negative human emotions that try to overwhelm us. If we didn't we'd go mad."

Follin considered this for a moment before asking another question. "If it really is that bad, why aren't you living with your parents in the Water Castle where it's safer?"

"That's because we aren't yet pure of spirit like they are and must breathe the air each day. We haven't evolved to the same level as the King and Queen. One day we'll need to escape this beauty you see around us. We'll miss it dearly," Jon's voice softened to a whisper. "But that is the price we pay for the beauty we experience on other planes of existence." Jon became silent and withdrawn.

Follin was stunned, he knew nothing of this. His understanding of energy and astral travel were all first hand. He had travelled on the wings of magic a thousand times.

"Why haven't I gone crazy then? I have these experiences all the time."

"One day you will need to escape... but then again..." Jon thought for a moment. "Maybe, just maybe you are immune. I don't know much about mages and their apprentices… perhaps you have something special that protects you, like the Archetypes."

Follin nodded his head in thought. "I hope so."

Jon stood suddenly, picked up his ale and finished it in one long swallow. "Come on, we should be getting ready for bed. We have a long ride tomorrow."

~

Follin's Meditation - Eight of Cups

Follin brought the picture of the Eight of Cups into his meditative space and immediately felt the man's restlessness. It seemed that this man also wished to leave on an adventure.

The eight cups formed a neat pattern but it was not quite complete, there was a gap in its arrangement. Follin thought that perhaps the man was fed up with trying to get them perfectly aligned, or maybe he was waiting for the very last cup to arrive.

"Look at it, go on, take a good long look, young man. That cup pattern is looking good enough for me. I've spent way too much time trying to get it just right, and now I'm fed up with it. I've decided to leave it as it is, to start out on a new adventure. I've wasted more than enough time on this stupid project and now I need a break." The man wrestled with his cloak as he stood up.

In a reckless, nervous manner he grabbed at his walking staff and set out on the road leading towards the mountains in the distance. "I've got rivers to cross and mountains to climb, and I'm going to enjoy it no matter what. Oh yes I am."

"Sir," said Follin, hurrying to keep up. "I see there is an eclipse in the sky, does that mean anything to you?"

"Of course it does, lad, you're studying astrology, can't you see that it's a Lunar Eclipse? It signals change, it's why I'm feeling so restless. It's calling me to end this project and start a new one. I've been so frustrated with it and this is the final straw. It means, 'time to move on, lad, move on, finish up, let it go and start a new project', that's what it says."

"But you've not finished this project, how can you move on and start a new one?"

"Lad, the eclipses urge us forwards, not backwards. This Eclipse signals an emotional ending. Besides, I'm feeling so much better now that I'm on the road again. Soon we'll have a Solar Eclipse and that's going to start something new, a new beginning."

Just then the man stopped and looked at Follin. "You there, young lad, you're on a journey too I see. What frustrations have you decided to leave behind?"

Follin sighed. "Yes, I suppose I have embarked on a new adventure. I leave the frustrations of trying to cope with my incessant worries and my wife's moods. Or maybe I'm trying to leave behind the horror of what happened in the Tarot Sanctuary." Follin thought for a moment then picked up a stick from the ground. "Hold on a second, sir. I've decided to join you on your journey. It seems that we both need to leave our burdens behind and start out on a new adventure."

Chapter 9 – Nine of Cups

Satisfaction, mentoring, life experience, good choices, earned wisdom.

After leaving Jon with his cousins at the Water Elf village the travellers headed east towards the dense oak forest that held Ziggy's Wood Elf clan. It was nestled close to Naroo's resting place on the River of Cups.

The rain came down in fits and spurts throughout their journey and, with the north wind driving the chill of the Hindamar Mountains, Follin soon complained that his clothing was always wet and he just felt miserable. When it was possible they stayed at the taverns, but once they left the Pilgrims Way there was no choice but to sleep in their makeshift shelters each night. It was with great relief that they finally reached the sanctity of the Wood Elf forests.

"Ziggy! Hail, to you and Follin, elf-wise!" came a firm but whispered voice. It originated from directly above Follin's head. He startled and looked up. High in a tree beside the track was an elf sentry, almost invisible in his dress of forest green. The elf quickly placed the arrow he had drawn back into its quiver. His handsome face beamed with happiness as he swung from bough to bough to finally land lightly on the ground. The elf sentry handed a small oak branch to Ziggy in greeting.

"Well met, brother." He turned to Follin and smiled. "Elf-wise, welcome, I am Pandjar." The middle-aged elf had three thick scars that ran deeply furrowed across his face. Follin couldn't help but wonder what manner of creature might have caused them.

"We've been watching for your arrival. The Wildlanders have been watching too. We startled two yesterday but they are back in greater numbers today. So please, Follin, do exactly what I do, be mindful of where you put your feet and be as quiet as a forest mouse." Pandjar reached down to Sox and petted his damp head. "And you, no running off. This be neither the time nor the place for gallivanting about in the forest."

The elf scout hastened to guide them along hidden paths that took them through dripping fern-lined gullies and leech-infested streams. If Follin had been well enough he would have enjoyed their trek over the slippery moss-covered rocks, along gullies so thick with ferns that their guide had to swing his long-bladed knife to clear a path for them. Twice they led their horses through waist-deep water to lose their tracks. All the while they remained silent. Each time Follin coughed, the elf scout put his finger to his lips signalling for him to be quiet. The normally exuberant Sox was subdued staying strictly on the path marked by their guide.

After many hours travelling hidden paths through the forest, the scarred elf eventually turned to Follin and pointed out several well-concealed archers high in the trees and said, "We are safe now, lad."

It was evening when they arrived at a clearing near the Wood Elf village. Here they were greeted by an excited crowd of elves who escorted them along a narrow, winding trail that led to their small, well-camouflaged huts of stone, timber and sod. Follin counted no more than forty elves. This was a small clan indeed, he thought.

Exhausted from having ridden in the wet and cold, Follin had saddle sores, a nasty cough and his nose wouldn't stop running. Not wanting to upset his hosts he put on a brave face and ignored his discomfort.

"This is Follin, elf-wise, of the Mystic Isle, apprentice magician to Mage Hermes of the Tarot Kingdom," announced Ziggy, introducing his friend to an old elven woman, behind her waited the rest of the clan.

"Elf-wise, I am Tataria, an elder of the Daru Wood Elves, and the clan healer. I am honoured to offer you our hearts and our homes as one of our own, a member of the Wood Elf Clan," she said stepping up to embrace their new clan member.

Pandjar, the scared, handsome elf who was their escort through the forest took Follin's hand in a friendly grasp. "Follin, welcome to our humble village. Brother Ziggy, may not have told you, but our clan is one of the oldest of this world. Unfortunately, there remain but few of us, hidden from the eyes of man in this grove of ancient oaks. Apart from our few Elf Ranger volunteers, it is rare for us to venture from the safety of our forests and the plains that stretch into the Swords Kingdom."

"Thank you, Tataria and Pandjar, for your kindness. I gladly pledge my honour, respect and loyalty to the Daru Wood Elf clan." Follin covered his mouth with his elbow and sneezed just as he finished.

"Our ways are simple, Follin, but please ask before requesting a gift or a service from us. We are generous people but our gifts can be two-edged…" Pandjar paused as his eyes wandered to Follin's sword strapped at his waist. At that moment his eyes lit up like the lanterns his people had strung out in welcome.

"Is that one of Master Pew's swords?" Pandjar asked in amazement. "And that looks like Master Lexis' scabbard."

Follin's face flushed in surprise and pride that this isolated band of Wood Elves would recognise his master's workmanship.

"Yes, they are," he said proudly as the curious elves crowded around him. "Would you like to hold it?" Follin asked unbuckling his sword and scabbard. He knew from experience that everyone who knew anything about blades would want to caress a sword made by Master Pew.

Pandjar did not immediately accept the proffered sword from his clan-mates outstretched hand. Instead, he looked at Follin and, turning to Ziggy, he raised his eyebrows in query. Pandjar was a warrior of renown. He had wielded many a weapon built with elven and elemental magic but seeing how Follin handed his sword so freely to a stranger gave him discomfort.

"Follin, how many magical swords did Master Pew make while you were apprenticed to him?"

Follin noticed that everyone went silent as they waited for his answer.

"I saw him make dozens of swords while I was with him. I helped make them."

"Well, my elf-wise friend," continued Pandjar. "This sword is of exceptional quality. Master Pew would die from exhaustion if he made more than one enchanted sword like this every twenty years. If he tried to make more his elementals would abandon him."

Follin was ready to argue the point but realised that this just might be true. "Why? He didn't seem to do anything different other than tell me and Justin to leave while he finished it."

"That's because he completed the magical passings with his elementals in secret. The fewer inquisitive eyes the better the outcome," replied the elf.

Pandjar continued. "Master Pew would only be able to make three or four swords like this in his entire lifetime, Follin. He must prepare himself and his elementals for years beforehand. You, my friend, are a very special person with a very special gift."

The elves crowded closer, anything of magic that came from the Tarot Empire was of enormous interest to beings where magic was a way of life.

After his explanation, Pandjar accepted Follin's sword and reverently drew the blade from its scabbard. A hush settled over the elves as they strained to gain a closer look.

"This be a work of beauty and wonder. I can feel your own hand in its making... but look here." Pandjar showed those closest the fine line of gold and silver worked into the blade. "This here is the seal of magic laid down by Master Pew and his elementals, see?"

"Yes, I know that, it's amazing isn't it." Follin had to raise his voice to be heard above the chattering of the elves. This started another fit of coughing. He rubbed at his running nose with the sleeve of his jacket having misplaced his rag in the confusion of arriving at the village. The elves straining to get a closer look at his sword soon forced Follin to the back of the crowd.

"Look here, Follin," called Pandjar. The elves politely made way for Follin to come back to the centre of the circle. "See this fine line, you have to look with eyes accustomed to magic. See how it shines so brightly? No, not the writing, it's these symbols, here and here... can you see them?"

Follin looked carefully but saw nothing. "No, I don't see anything other than Master Pew's seal," came his disappointed reply.

Pandjar motioned for Follin to come closer. When within arm's reach the elven warrior placed his hand on Follin's forehead. Holding it there for several seconds he said, "Now have a look and tell us what you see."

Follin's eyes lit up as a blast of hot energy exploded in his third eye.

"Wow!" he cried in wonder, "this blade is alive, I can see its life force. And there, there are the enchanted symbols, they move and swirl. Please, pass me Master Lexis' leather scabbard. I want to see what the leather master did to it," Follin was ecstatic. As he grasped the scabbard it shone as though it too were alive. The light encased his entire body in a dazzling aura.

Follin's smile was almost brighter than the scabbard's. "This is truly a gift of magic. Why didn't Master Pew tell me?"

Pandjar laughed lightly, the scars that ran across his face stood out in the lamplight. "Follin, sometimes a gift's power is best discovered when it is most needed. I am saddened to tell you that the time is fast approaching when you will be called upon to use this sword for what it was created. I sense that many souls will be sent to the Shadowlands at the edge of this blade."

Follin rubbed gently at his forehead where the elf had put his hand. "Pandjar, your energy is really powerful. I've not experienced that kind of energy before, what is it?" he asked, bewildered that Pandjar's energy was so different to Ziggy's.

"That be mountain lion magic, lad, one of the many forms of fire magic. I claimed it many years ago." Pandjar's fingers unconsciously stroked the puckered scars on his cheek. "I was attacked by a band of mountain lions many years ago, a time when most animals could still talk. To stop my bleeding I was forced to snatch some of their energy while a dear friend kept them from ripping me apart. At that moment I was blessed with some interesting lion traits that I draw upon for fighting and healing. I kind of like their energy too. Perhaps one day I'll tell you the story of the lions of the Hindamar Mountains and the folly of Pandjar who sought to beg a seed from the Mother of Oaks. By the way, that giant oak shading our camp is from the very seed that almost cost me my life that day."

Within an hour of their arrival, Follin had developed a fever and was soon put to bed. Sox sat at his master's bedside, his eyes never leaving Follin's face. With a worried frown, Tataria, the clan healer, took pains to boil a special fusion of herbs to reduce his fever.

"I've planned this trip for months and now Follin is laid low by a common cold. I fear that our charge is wandering the astral planes like a living wraith," grunted Ziggy sourly, disappointed that he was unable to help his friend.

"Sox has followed him in his wanderings and will keep him safe," stated Pandjar.

"I'm worried that Follin might not come back from his wanderings. He's disoriented, and there's something else happening here I don't understand." Tataria's voice shook slightly as she lifted Follin's head to dribble some of her herbal remedy between his dry lips. "I know that it is extremely unsafe for us elves to go wandering in the Shadowlands, but someone will need to cross over and rescue him. My herbs and energy work has stabilised his fever, to a degree, but if he doesn't break his fever tonight I am fearful he will step beyond our reach. I believe that this is more than a simple fever."

Late that evening the group sat on cushions around Follin's bed. Tataria turned to her cousin, Ziggy, and lifted the corner of one eye in question.

"It is arranged," Ziggy said softly. "He will be there when we need him." His face softened for just a second as he smiled - it was a cold, grim smile.

Tataria placed a clay dish on top of the fire in the middle of the hut. Reaching into a leather bag she withdrew a mix of herbs and fungi which she threw into the dish. The room filled with the refreshing fragrances of pennyroyal, rue, mugwort, lavender and other earthy scents.

One-by-one Ziggy, Pandjar and Tataria closed their eyes to gather at the very edge of the Shadowlands. Follin's physical form was in the hut with them but his astral body was wandering in the gloom of the land of the dead.

"Sox, find Follin," ordered Tataria.

It was quiet there, no sound, no movement, and it was cold. Sox whimpered as he sniffed the air - his master had disappeared. There now appeared many creatures wandering towards Sox through the mist, lost souls trapped by some unseen force, attracted by the opening made by the elves' magic. With a yelp of anger Sox leapt at several dark shapes.

"Someone must be using them, enlivening them," Tataria whispered softly. "The poor souls, they're more terrified of us than we are of them." The shadowy forms continued to drift about in the gloom. Those that came too close were quickly chased off by Sox.

Suddenly both Sox and Tataria stiffened. "I can sense Follin, he is close," she warned, "so does Sox. He was frightened and has placed a shield of invisibility around himself. It's protecting him from the lost souls."

Tataria bent and placed her forehead on Sox's. "Sox, your master is close, very close," she whispered as she raised her vibration to isolate and dispel Follin's shield of invisibility.

Sox slowly walked in a circle to eventually stop at a grey shape on the ground that no one had noticed earlier. With several soft yaps of joy, he dragged at what appeared to be a blanket beneath which lay Follin. His body was cold and lifeless beneath the covering. Sox licked his master's face but there was no response.

"Ziggy, is he here yet?" asked Tataria.

Ziggy nodded just as a dark presence approached them in the gloom. Sox immediately sensed the figure and barked, but it was a strange bark that the guardians felt was more of joy than a warning. Three more sharp, fae barks and the gloom cleared to reveal that the figure was indeed human.

The man was tall, aged but had a youthful step. He walked in haste as though desperate to get to them.

"Where is he? The Hierophant said I would find him in this direction," the stranger cried in a hurried, almost panicked voice. When he saw the shape huddled on the ground the man dropped to his knees and shook the cold body.

"Follin? Son! Wake up, it's me, Da."

At the sound of his father's voice, Follin's eyes suddenly darted open and he sat upright.

"Da? Da? Is that you, Da?"

"Yes, son, it's me." Follin's father, Mage Saoirse, bent and lifted Follin in his arms and the two hugged.

"Da! I missed you," Follin sobbed, his face wet with tears of joy.

"Son, I am sorry. I can't tell you how sorry I am that I had to leave you." The Mage's voice was strained with emotion. "Son, I'm taking you out of this place, it's not safe for you to be here." In the space of a heartbeat, they were in Tataria's hut.

When Follin awoke he found himself lying on Tataria's bed. His father stood above him, and, raising the wooden wand in his hand, he caught the light of Tataria's lamp with its crystal tip.

Breathing deeply the Mage pointed to Follin's navel centre with his left hand. With his right, he stretched to point his wand upwards towards the heavens. A sudden blast of radiant light suffused Follin's body causing him to jolt upright with the shock of its entry.

The Mage helped his son lie back in the bed, then pulled a dagger from his coat to place it in Follin's right hand. "With this Dagger, your mind will clear and you will banish the spell that sickened and confused you."

He next took out a small, golden cup and placed it in his son's left hand. "With this Cup, your joyful nature will return. Your heart will fill with a love of life and of all living creatures."

Next, the Mage took a large gold coin and placed it at Follin's feet. "With this Coin, your spirit will embed firmly in the earth and you will feel the desire to place your feet on the soil of your family home."

The old mage finally placed his wand on Follin's chest and pulled the rug over his son's sleeping body. "With this Wand, your power will return so that you can fulfil your destiny."

The Mage finally bent down to hug the fae dog at his son's bedside. Sox joyfully licked his face before lying down with one eye open, watching the group slowly file out into the dawn light.

"He is safe, and now we can eat, I'm starved!" announced Follin's father as he gratefully accepted a bowl of spiced potato and cabbage soup.

"Mage Saoirse..." began Pandjar.

He was interrupted by the Mage speaking through a mouth full of food. "Pandjar, please, call me Sao, I haven't grown into a foggy old man yet you know."

Pandjar smiled. "Ah, yes, I had forgotten old friend. Sao, can you tell us what may have caused your son's illness?"

"Follin's spirit was weakened after travelling in the rain, that's quite natural, of course. I also suspect that he lost some of his vital force in dispersing the Wildlander mage's search-spells." Mage Saoirse sipped at his tea and, tearing off a piece of bread, dipped it into his bowl. Closing his eyes he savoured the aromatic flavours. "Ah, I so miss these elven meals," he said wiping his bowl clean with the last of his bread.

He continued. "Those mages hold total control over the tribes north of the Wands Kingdom and the Hindamar Mountains. Such is their power that they have broken the traditions of honour that the Wildlanders have held for thousands of years. I know this because I spent many years travelling through the Wildlands and beyond. Some of those scoundrel mages have even crossed into the Shadowlands to command the lost souls wandering about there. Cruel, that's what it is, just cruel."

Pandjar slurped from his own bowl and said, "Sao, remember how we talked about that rogue band of mages years ago when we were in the Wands hospice, the one beside Kwadinsa's shrine? I can't remember its name... anyway, you said back then that they were trying to buy dragon magic."

"Yes, yes, I do remember. We were trying to work out what those black-hearted mages were up to. I now know part of the story." The elves leaned in closer to listen. "That group of mages travelled through lands that I hadn't even heard of. They finally found someone willing to tell them the secret of how to obtain dragon magic, it is dangerous but it can be done. A dragon's magic is not evil as such, but it can be deadly and almost impossible to detect and even more difficult to counteract."

"Dragon magic, aye, the oldest magic in the land. Maybe that's why we had so much trouble trying to help Hera," mused Ziggy.

"I fear that those evil mage's knowledge of aberrant forms of magic has also contributed to my son's illness," continued the Mage.

By mid-afternoon Follin was well enough to sit up in his bed, his fever gone. It was time to talk, father to son.

"Da, I think I saw you in my meditations not so long ago. You were only young, an apprentice mage in Pan's cave. You were undergoing a test, just as I did," Follin began.

Sao thought for a moment then smiled. "Yes, I remember a young man in Pan's cave when I undertook that test. I had no idea who it was - so it was you? How this could be I don't know. I was quite young when Pan called for me, I had only just married too." The Mage chuckled. "Son, would you like to know which cup I chose when Pan called me back the second time?"

It was Follin's turn to smile. "I already know, you didn't choose any of them."

His father laughed out loud. "Aye, you are too much like me. I told Pan I wasn't interested in gifts. I told him I wished to earn my powers. Now, what did you choose when Pan tested you?"

"Guess," challenged Follin with a grin.

The Mage grunted in delight. "I knew it! We're both tarred with the same brush, stubborn as mules and not interested in handouts. You will make a fine magician, son," he said proudly. Mage Saoirse stopped laughing and went quiet. He had things he wanted to say and the burden of guilt he carried called for its release.

"I don't know how much you remember, but I want to tell you of my leaving, I owe it to you," said the Mage as he eased his lean frame to sit on the bed beside his son.

"Da, I was little, I remember some but not much. I missed you so much I cried myself to sleep every night for years." When Follin looked at his father he saw tears in the old man's eyes.

"That was a terrible time, son. The marauding Wildlanders caught us by surprise. Our soldiers tried their best to protect the villages but it was too late for many of them. I was called on to help the injured and was given a healing tent in the north-west of the isle. The Wildlanders were finally defeated in a large battle, but as they retreated to their boats they left behind the plague."

He nodded as though to himself then closed his eyes as images of the horror of those times flooded his mind.

"I was busy healing the wounded when the plague struck. I worked day and night, scouring the woods for herbs and drawing on my healing skills to the point of exhaustion. One night I fell asleep at the bedside of one of my patients and, without realising it, I remote viewed our village of Saoirse. I went to our home where I saw that the plague had entered my own household, it had a stranglehold on Evert, your older brother. I knew that I had to leave, I had to go home before it spread to the rest of my family." He paused to wipe at the tears on his cheeks.

"I immediately awoke, packed my few belongings together and started running. There were no horses available, they had been requisitioned by the army. As I ran I projected my mind forward to spy for the special healing herbs I would need. I ran for five days only stopping to sleep a few hours each night. I managed to put up a protective shield around my family so that it would help protect you from the ravages of the plague." Mage Saoirse became silent and stopped. A choked sob escaped his lips and his face creased into a mask of grief.

"But my power was fading and I had to decide which of my beautiful family I must leave to die." Hot tears spilled down his shirt front as he tried to continue with the story but his grief was too great. Follin silently waited, both hands holding tightly to his father's.

"My beautiful firstborn, Evert, I knew I couldn't save him. The famous Mage of Saoirse; Astrologer and Seer of the Mystic Isle; the Dragon Mage; Healer of the Hindamar Highlands; Master Mage of the Northwest Wildlands!" He spat it out as though the words burnt his tongue. "I was famous for my healing and yet I could not save my own son."

He wiped the sleeve of his cloak across his face as bitter tears fell afresh. "I decided to save you, your sister, Theresa and your mother. It was the hardest decision of my life, yet, I do not regret it. I can honestly say I loved you all equally. While I slept I was forced to watch Evert draw closer to the Shadowlands. When I woke I ran faster. My shoes soon fell apart so I wrapped my shirt around my feet. When the cloth tore away I tied bark from the trees for my footwear. When my bark shoes disintegrated I ran barefoot along the paths. My feet had become a mass of bloody flesh. When I arrived home my swollen feet oozed blood and pus much like a plague victim's corpse. My body was emasculated and I collapsed through the front door.

"In my unconscious state, I could see Evert approaching the land of Shadows. When he saw me he smiled and waved. Before I could catch up to him he had crossed into the land beyond time and space. I knew that one step nearer and I too would be lost to this world. I saw Evert turn to a sound from the mist of rainbows which separates life from death. I can see him now, his face lit up as hands reached out to hold him. I glimpsed my family, relatives and friends who had passed on. They beckoned for me to follow, but Evert had gone. When I awoke in the morning I was bathed and my wounds dressed. Your mother was asleep in the chair at my feet as you and Theresa played by the fireplace. Evert was in his bed yet there was no breath in his lungs." Mage Sao sat silently, his hands twisted as though in pain. He could no longer speak, stuck at a place in time, a time when his life seemed to have ended.

"Da? What's the Shadowlands like? Did Evert like it?" asked Follin, trying to keep his father from dwelling on such dark thoughts.

"Aye, 'tis beautiful. Mage Hermes once told me a story of how dangerous the rainbow mist of the Shadowlands is for a mage. He likened it to being with his first love. When Hermes was twenty-one years of age he fell in love with a sweet lass of seventeen. He had been placed in a small village in the Cups Kingdom to study under a famous Cups healer. All that summer they made love. His heart soared like an eagle at the very sight and scent of that beautiful girl. Whenever he visits the Shadowlands that same heady euphoria of young love draws him deeper. He is fearful that one day he won't come back. That's why mages only approach the Shadowlands with someone to help them, like your elves and The Hierophant did for me last night. Very rarely does a mage wander those lands alone, many have gone there and never returned. It is even more dangerous for elves, you will rarely hear of an elf who has crossed and returned from such a journey."

The Mage continued. "Son, in the Shadowlands I experienced exactly what Mage Hermes described. Evert was so happy and I wished that I could die and join him such was the pain in my heart. But then you came to me. You had stepped into the Shadowlands all by yourself, just ten years of age. You took me by the hand and pulled me back from the edge. If you had not been there I would not have been able to return of my own accord."

Follin sat silently tossing this over in his mind. "All I remember, Da, is you and I digging the hole for Evert. It was raining and you were crying. I saw the bandages slowly unwinding from around your swollen feet. I watched as your blood mixed with the mud and flowed into Evert's grave."

"That was a bad day, son. It took me months to recover my physical health, but my soul, it remained a suppurating wound. That wound turned into a restless urge to escape the torture of the images of my eldest son's death. The guilt and shame I felt at having sacrificed one of my own children took hold of me. I wrestled every night with my inner demons. I cried by day and I screamed at night in my sleep. Your poor mother couldn't take it any longer. She had her own grief to manage plus two small children. In the end, she ordered me to leave, to heal myself. Your wise mother handed me my walking staff, my bag of magic and told me not to come back until I was healed."

"Da, I didn't know that. Where did you go?"

"Everywhere, nowhere... I travelled the world and eventually ended up on Runda Isle. That was where I was able to heal my spirit."

Follin stared at his father. "The Isle of Secrets? Why did you go there, Da?"

"It was my destiny, son. Our bloodline goes back to the Runda Isle elementals much like the kings and queens of each Tarot Kingdom. I learned that our forefathers wandered the ocean looking for a safe home. They feared a repeat of the horror of what the pirates had done to our ancestors. They thought they would find it on the Mystic Isle, your birthplace. The invasions from the Wildlanders demonstrated that it wasn't in our destiny to run and hide."

"But did you heal, Da? Did the mages on Runda Isle heal you?"

"There are no mages on Runda Isle. I sat with the elementals and learned their secrets. Over time I came to terms with my guilt and shame."

"But what about Ma and Theresa, what happened to them?"

"I took a ship to the City of Life and then to the Mystic Isle. I took your mother and sister to live with me on Runda Isle while you were sojourning with the Archetypes of the Major Arcana. I now realise that I should have told Sir Cecil, it would have saved you a lot of grief. We spent some years on Runda Isle but then your mother wanted to see the dragons, but that is another story, son. Your mother and sister are safe, living happily in our home in the Wands Kingdom."

Follin's face lit up. "Does that mean I'll see dragons when I bring my family to visit Ma in the Wands Kingdom?"

Through fresh tears Mage Saoirse answered, "Son, that's why I'm here. When The Hierophant appeared at our house your mother handed me my swag of magic and showed me the door. She said, *'and don't come back without Follin and his family!'*"

~

Follin's Meditation - Nine of Cups

Follin entered the ninth picture which consisted of a man sitting in front of a series of cups set out on display, like trophies. 'This looks interesting, it makes me feel that I have just about everything I need in life. I have a happy life, a wife and two children on their way. My father is back in my life and my sister and mother are safe and I'll see them soon.'

He shifted his perspective and spoke to the man in the picture.

"Sir, can you please explain the lesson of this image?"

The man stood and turned to admire the cups sitting displayed in a row behind him. "Certainly I can. These cups signify the successes in my life. They demonstrate that I have made some wise decisions over the years. I well knew, though, that I might also lose everything, for such are the vagaries of life. To honour my success I make an effort to teach others who wish to know how I have come to be in so fortunate a position."

Follin's eyes brightened. "So, you know the secret of success? I'd like to hear that, if I may."

The man leaned towards Follin and whispered. "These trophies are the result of years of trial and error. As each system failed I learned something, I learned what not to do. I also found that my chances of success improved when I listened to what my wise elders had to say. I matured and learned to adjust my expectations. I set simpler goals, took one step at a time, knowing that when I tried to skip a few steps there was always the possibility of failure.

"I also spoke to those who had expertise in their field. I went to their workplace and volunteered my time to help them. My honest and humble approach was appreciated by my mentors. I now teach others on their path so as to give back to my community. My success is simply the result of hard work and being genuine with people, that is what makes 'lady luck' smile upon you. Don't take shortcuts or cheat to get ahead. Don't gamble beyond what you are prepared to answer to your wife for. In all things strive to be honourable and respectful with those you meet."

"Is that it? I don't mean to be rude or disrespectful but, that's rather simplistic."

As Follin was speaking the man changed into the Justice Lady. "Follin, it is simple. Don't lie, steal or cheat and above all be honest with yourself for that is the way. It is foolhardy to think that success is a secret, because it isn't."

Chapter 10 – Ten of Cups

Success, happy family, community, contentment.

Later that week Ziggy, Pandjar, Tataria, Follin and the Mage of Saoirse, sat comfortably on the cushions in Tataria's hut.

"Follin," said Ziggy. "As you know, I have unfinished business to attend to, but first I need to explain why I have chosen you to assist me in finding my family. Of all the people I am close to, you are the one I believe can help me do what others consider impossible.

"My wife, Sorcha, and I, always wanted to have children. As the years passed and the fighting with the Wildlanders escalated we decided to wait before starting a family. Sorcha had a warm but fragile heart and was often unwell but by some mischance, she fell pregnant. It was a miracle that lit us from within and the joy I saw on her face each morning made me as happy as one could be. As the pregnancy progressed, however, I grew afraid for Sorcha and our child's welfare. As you know, I serve with the Elven Rangers, doing my duty to help protect the Tarot Empire and my people. When our leader, Ellistar, was killed in an ambush, I was asked to take his place as our squad's captain.

"Our first child, Tamotar, is a bright boy, dearly cherished by our clan. He was the first child born to both Wood and Water elves for many hundreds of years, everyone in the clans spoiled him. Then along came Lily, she was as beautiful as the flower she was named after. We knew she would be our last child for elves fear mortality. We know that a child brought into this world must endure the harsh realities of pain and suffering.

"After Lily was born Sorcha grew fragile with the arduous responsibilities of motherhood in a precarious world. It became necessary for my family to stay with Sorcha's Water Elf clan when I went on patrol with the Rangers. These were not Ardler and Carlia's clan, but another which had remained hidden deep in the eastern boglands of the Cups Kingdom. Her family were delicate souls yet they were held in high regard for their healing magic. We knew that everyone in the clan would selflessly sacrifice their lives to protect our children.

"It was at this time that I was sent on a mission beyond the Wands Kingdom to help subdue a rogue band of Wildlander mages. I was accompanied by my brother, Pandjar, and other elves of similar experience. Pandjar is a fierce fighter and has made many enemies among the Wildlanders and especially their mages."

"Ziggy, when did this happen?" Follin asked softly, not wishing to interrupt Ziggy's explanation.

"These events happened while you were quite young. It was at the same time your father lost his eldest, your brother, Evert."

That shocked Follin. "So this happened only about fifteen years ago?"

"Yes, that's correct." Ziggy returned to his story. "While we were fighting I believed that my wife and children would be safely hidden deep in the boglands protected by Sorcha's clan. When we have need, elves are ferocious warriors, and her people were as brave and fierce as any elf. However, I didn't reckon on the cunning savagery of the Wildlander mages. They discovered Sorcha's village and violated its sanctuary in retaliation for our Ranger's fighting prowess."

Ziggy stopped speaking for a moment. When he next spoke his voice was bitter with emotion. "My wife's clan fought like devils but, being few in number, they were soon overcome. Those the mages didn't kill they used for their cruel magical purposes. Sorcha and my children had been gathering herbs in the boglands, but when they returned to the village they were captured." Ziggy suddenly stopped and a sob broke from his lips. The elf quickly closed his eyes and sipped at the tea Tataria handed him to calm his grief.

"Follin, this tragedy was very hard on all of us," said Tataria in her soft, melodic voice, breaking the tension of the moment. "I was on my way to visit Sorcha and the children when I came across their devastated village. When I saw that the Water Elf clan had been wiped out, I called for Ziggy to return home."

"I sensed what had happened but couldn't prevent it. I came home as fast as I could but my wife and children had disappeared. For some reason, we were unable to locate where the mages had taken them and to this day we still don't know." The grief he felt was evident in his red-rimmed eyes as he turned to stare into the fire.

"In my despair, I went into the Shadowlands with the intention of finding where they might be, something, anything, but the signs were hidden. The Shadowlands are filled with blackness and there is no order or form to guide the unwary. In my grief, I soon became disoriented and lost. Few elves have been foolish enough to attempt this journey, and even fewer return." Ziggy paused as he softly placed his hand on Follin's shoulder.

"It was there that I met you, a small boy with special powers leading his father to safety. You had somehow followed your father into the Shadowlands to rescue him. It was on your return that you found me. I was lost and had begun to will myself to die. You took me by the hand and led me back to the land of the living. When we parted you said that one day you would return to help me find my family. And that, my friend, is why I have asked you to attend me on this journey."

The small group watched as a dawning awareness lit Follin's face. He closed his eyes and in a light trance, he began to speak, recalling that event.

"I remember now, yes, I can see you! I, I was holding my father's hand and very mindful not to let go when I reached down to take yours. Your hand was so light, there was almost no life in you. I knew I couldn't let go of my Da's hand because he would have wandered away. I didn't know what to do with you, I too was lost. Then something strange happened. I saw a white dog in the distance and as it barked a bright light lit up the darkness, it was a beacon. I think that dog must have been Sox, or perhaps one of his kin, who showed me the way home."

Ziggy reached down and scratched Sox under his chin. "What a mysterious world we live in, Follin. It appears that your fae dog can travel through time as well as space. That is uncommon but not unknown with the fae." Ziggy stared into the fire for a moment then turned to look into his friend's eyes. "Follin, Tataria assures us that you are well enough for this undertaking. I am now asking you, as my elf-wise brother, to fulfil your promise to help me find my family.

"Of course I am well enough," Follin exclaimed. "We will find your family if it is destined."

Mage Saoirse believed that Follin would be able to use Sox's fae powers in the Shadowlands in their endeavour to locate Sorcha and the children. Closing his eyes Follin engaged with the combined energy of the group. Moments later he and Sox found themselves between the worlds of mankind and the etheric plains - the Shadowlands.

Guided by the Mage's soft voice, Follin looked around to orient himself before following Sox into the gloom. Within a few minutes, he found himself staring at a series of low, brush-covered hills covered in a thick fog. He paused as he tried to assemble the shifting images as one reality was superimposed upon the other. He recognised that he was neither in this world nor the

Shadowlands, he was in both at the same time. It felt strange for Follin but didn't seem to bother Sox in the least.

There was a barrier in the distance, much like a waterfall, lit by a brilliant rainbow. The landscape below him was populated by people, no doubt these were the newly-dead, he thought. He watched in fascination as they spontaneously appeared, some in groups, some individually. As soon as they appeared they would begin to walk towards the rainbow mist which flashed brightly as each stepped into it. There was a vague familiarity about the rainbow, an old memory perhaps, but he couldn't recall what it was.

Sox yapped in joy then began jogging purposefully up the hill causing the images of rainbows and the dead to disappeared. Within moments they were forced to slow as the mist deepened. Before long all Follin could see of his dog was his white fur coat. Sox appeared to be floating, his black socks were indistinguishable from the darkness of the ground he was running over.

The path grew steeper until they were halted by a cliff face. There appeared to be no way over or around, even Sox stopped. Sniffing the ground he let out a low growl.

"Sox, is this the way to Sorcha and Ziggy's children?" asked Follin.

Sox's bark was answer enough.

"Is there danger?"

Sox replied with a simple snarled warning and Follin sensed the presence of the Wildlander's evil mages.

"Can you find Sorcha?"

Sox gave an excited bark, it was bright with hope and happiness. The mist began to clear with each of Sox's barks. Slowly an image of a lightly forested valley appeared, on one side was a small cave. Outside that cave sat three elves, a woman and two children. Follin felt a bolt of awareness pulse through his body. At that moment he knew what had happened the day the Wildlander mages invaded Sorcha's Water Elf village.

When Follin returned to consciousness he quickly described the forested hill and the cave.

"I knew they weren't dead! I know that place too, it's in the hills opposite Naroo's resting place. My family have been living right under our noses all this time!" Ziggy shook his head from side to side in amazement, his voice thick with emotion.

Follin continued with his report. "Ziggy, I saw what Sorcha did. She tricked the mages into passing right next to Naroo's resting place. I felt a strange intertwining of elemental and elven magic there and all around the cave. Sorcha activated this magic so that she could escape to the cave with the children. The Wildlander mages know that Sorcha is there, somewhere, and they know that we are searching for her right now. Ziggy, they are waiting for us."

On hearing this news Ziggy forced a grim smile. "My marvellous wife has made a sanctuary in the midst of such evil." He pulled his blade free of its scabbard and declared, "You and I have a destiny that demands fulfilment. Blood will flow but it will not be ours, I promise it."

He turned to Follin's father who had been silent throughout the meeting. "Mage Sao, I wish for your blessing on our journey."

The Mage acknowledged his old friend. "Ziggy, it is my honour to offer you my blessing on this quest. I am too old to accompany you, but I shall make my magic available to Follin if he needs it."

Pandjar stood and clasped the hands of both Follin and his brother. As he bid them goodnight he reached into his pocket and pulled out a soft leather pouch which he handed to Ziggy.

"I see that you are down to the last of your leaf, brother. This is a pouch of very rare Water Elf tobacco, it comes straight from our bogland cousins. We shall enjoy a pipe together on your return."

Tataria also had gifts. A white cloth bag of herbs for Follin's cold, and to Ziggy she handed a beautiful cloth and straw child's doll, and a bag of small wooden balls.

"One never knows when a gift such as these might come in handy."

~

At dawn the next morning the small band quietly slipped across the River of Cups and into the forested hills beyond. Ziggy watched as Pandjar carefully placed his scouts near Naroo's resting place to ensure their safe return. The two set off at a slow jog as Sox led them across the shallow river ford and then along a narrow track that led deep into the forested hills.

After a short time they rounded a bend in the forest track which opened into a clearing ringed by a high wall of rock, it appeared very much like a fighting arena. As they reached the midpoint of the grassed area they were shocked into immobility by the sound of laughter. A band of Wildlander mages were standing on a rock ledge above them. Each was dressed in a grey cloak and held a staff in one hand. From the forest, they saw an army of Wildlander warriors blocking their retreat.

"We're trapped! Those vipers on the ledge are controlling these warriors. Look, that one, the leader, that's Mage Armitar, he is the vilest of them all. How he survived death at the hands of Londar's Brown-cap archers I don't know," grunted Ziggy pulling his bright elven sword from its scabbard. "Unsheathe thy enchanted sword, elf-wise, it is time for battle!"

Follin reacted immediately. Regretting his decision not to bring his bow and quiver, he drew his sword from its scabbard. This was the first time he had been required to wield it in defence of those he loved. A wave of euphoria immediately erupted along his arm, his body pulsed with the forces woven into the sword and scabbard.

With a flick of their wrists, Follin and Ziggy swung their swords above their heads as they adopted a fighting stance in preparation for battle. Neither noticed that Sox showed no interest in the Wildlander warriors stalking towards them. His gaze was fixed on the band of mages directing the Wildlanders into battle from the rock ledge above.

Ziggy adjusted the grip on his sword handle as he planted his feet wide. He turned and saw that Follin had adopted a similar fighting posture, and a tight smile momentarily flitted across his face. In that brief moment, Ziggy saw that his companion possessed qualities he had not seen before. His Mystic Isle friend was a novice no longer, but a master swordsman - this was Follin's coming of age.

As Follin gazed towards the enemy warriors he felt something began to stir within his breast. It awoke a memory from many years previously when he was initiated into Pan's magic. In a flash of insight, Follin realised that the energy of the four elements heavily dominated this place.

'Naroo's magical weavings are strong here,' he thought.

He could now see how Naroo, in her dying moments, had used her elven magic to weave a protective shield around her brave rescuer, the young Frailbones. Naroo's gift to her courageous rescuer was a cloak of invisibility, fortitude and protection from the Wildlander's missiles. It ensured Frailbone's survival, yet the effort drained the last ounce of life from her. In that split second of awareness Follin saw Pan, his face drawn and tear-streaked by the loss of one of his favourite beings, take Naroo's magical weavings and bind them to the four elements. He spun Naroo's gift to Frailbones into a permanent sanctuary for all beings seeking safety from evil.

Without thinking Follin instinctively melded with the forest as he had done with the Pentacles in their fight with the Wildlanders. Not having enough power of his own to stop these fierce warriors Follin engaged the forest to spread a sense of foreboding among the enemy.

"We fight together, brother," he heard Ziggy call, his voice sounding harsh in the still morning air. "Be careful and keep your back to the cliff wall." Ziggy slipped into his Elf Ranger mode and was in total control. "If we survive their charge we'll try to climb these rocks and attack the mages. If we can't do that we'll try to gain the higher ground to our right – I can see no other way." Ziggy's handsome face was strained and beads of sweat had formed on his brow.

"Ziggy, take heart, some of those mages on the ledge are not of the living, they have limited power here," shouted Follin just as the Wildlanders let loose their battle cry and charged towards them. Instinctively Follin adopted a different stance as he felt his mind fuse with Pan's forest elemental's and Naroo's elven web.

As the enemy came within killing range Follin and the Wood Elf leapt forward. Ziggy swung his sword to slice the head from the closest warrior's shoulders - the battle had begun.

Follin automatically began Sir Rohan's Dolphin Warrior fighting style. His movements were fluid giving him total command of his personal space - parrying, twisting, ducking and spinning, to lay his sword tip or blade on his enemy. Ziggy, in contrast, was a whirlwind, a deadly, destructive force. His body did not remain still for a single heartbeat as he swung his blade skillfully disposing of those trying to overwhelm them.

Follin was in a state that he could only describe as ecstasy. He wielded his sword with a light stroke that created a state of blind panic to enter his enemy's mind. The Wildlander warrior would suddenly freeze in fear then turn to race towards the forest screaming in terror. As Follin and Ziggy dispatched their foes the Wildlander mages above them began to feel a panic of their own - Follin's magic was routing their army.

"Follin, what are you doing?" whispered Ziggy as the first wave of Wildlanders raced away in panic. The next wave of warriors could be seen hesitating, afraid of the two devil warriors opposite them.

"I have aligned myself with the magic that Naroo weaved here before she died. Pan helped her create an uncommon fusion of elemental and elven magic, and it surrounds us now. It's beyond the mage's ability to tear it apart," answered Follin, his chest rising and falling as he breathed deeply. "All I need do, Ziggy, is touch my sword to my opponent and it fills them with a stupefying panic."

Ziggy dared to glance at his friend. "You fill me with hope, elf-wise. Let us finish this and dispatch these Wildlanders once and for all. I am weary of waiting and have a mighty yearning to embrace my family." Follin had only known the elf to wear the furrowed brow of grief, but he now saw that it had been replaced by an expression of joyful expectation.

Despite the battle that raged around him Sox had yet to move. He stood alert, like a statue, his gaze fixed on the group of mages on the ledge above. His nose twitched and his lips lifted momentarily into a low snarl.

When the Wildlanders fled back into the forest, the warriors in the second wave hesitated. They were terrified having just witnessed their brothers abandon the fight in a delirious panic. Across the field of battle lay discarded weapons, shields, pieces of armour, and even leather sandals to lend the terror-stricken Wildlanders greater speed as they sought to escape.

When it appeared that Follin and Ziggy would completely rout their army, the confused and frustrated mages lifted their staffs in an attempt to instil within their warriors the will to fight. Sox had been waiting for this moment. With the agility that only a fae dog could command, Sox leapt onto the ledge and with a frightening howl began to savage the mages.

Immediately Mage Armitar disappeared in an explosion of vile, black smoke. The other mages baulked and collided against each other as they tried to fend off the ferocious dog. The power they wielded over their warriors now completely collapsed as many of the mages also exploded in clouds of black smoke and disappeared. As if by command the remaining Wildlander warriors turned and fled back towards the forest as though summoned by a magical piper.

Follin wiped at the sweat from his brow as he watched Sox chase the last few mages along the ledge. Ziggy quickly positioned himself to intercept those who tried to leap to safety. A series of dull bursts of smoke and the last wicked mage was dispatched. With their demise came a single bark of joy as Sox leapt off the ledge. Stretching to his full height he licked Follin's face.

"You are such a good boy!" Follin said as Sox barked in delight.

Ziggy, though, had sagged to the ground placing his face in his hands. His body shook with the release of long-suppressed emotion. Follin put his arm around his elven friend's shoulders and Sox licked Ziggy's face. The three sat quietly to recover from the ferocity of battle. They sat quietly until they had recovered before resuming their journey to find Sorcha's cave.

Only a few minutes later an excited Sox surged forward to race into a particularly thick patch of mist. The dog barked several times forcing the mist to lift revealing the entrance to a small cave. As Sox ran towards the cave a woman and two children came out to greet him.

Ziggy's breath burst from his lips in a stifled cry and he began to run, stumbling in the thick patches of coarse grass.

"Sorcha! Sorcha!" he sobbed.

The woman and her children stopped to peer into the mist. Running towards them they saw two men dressed for battle - warriors! Fear now replaced joy as the three turned to run back into their cave.

"Sorcha! It's me, Ziggy!" the elf screamed in despair.

One by one the three stopped running to stare at the two warriors.

"Da, is that you?" came a child's curious voice.

"Yes, it's me, I've come for you," sobbed Ziggy as he embraced his oldest child. "Tamotar, I missed you so." Reaching to draw his daughter to him he said, "Lily, my sweetheart, you are safe now."

"Darling, what took you so long? You've been gone all day. Did you bring anything for the children?" came the soft, enchanting voice of Sorcha. Follin saw that she was thin, too thin, yet she was beautiful. She smiled but there was trepidation hiding behind it.

"Oh, you've brought a friend," she said when she noticed Follin standing patiently beside Sox. Nodding to him she said, "Please join us, I sense that you are elf-wise of the Wood Elf Clan. I've prepared a meal for my husband but there's enough for all of us." Sorcha turned and waved with her hand inviting the two men to enter her home. By the comfortable manner the family behaved around Sox, Follin realised that his dog must have been a regular visitor.

The cave was stark. It had a dirt floor, the earthen walls smelled of dampness, spider webs and thin tree roots dangled from the ceiling. An earthy odour hung in the air. Sorcha moved effortlessly around the cave preparing an invisible meal. She was performing an elaborate pantomime, gesturing with her hands at the various imaginary dishes on an imaginary table.

"Please, help yourself to the food while I prepare a bed for you, elf-wise." Again she moved around invisible obstacles to make up a bed on an imaginary couch.

Follin looked awkwardly at his friend who had sagged to his knees on the floor, tears of despair coursing down his cheeks. Ziggy said nothing, he was powerless to do any more than be a passive participant in his wife's delusions.

There was a sudden, sharp bark. Sox looked at the woman and barked again, and then again. With each bark, the cave took the shape of Ziggy's hut in the nearby elven village. There now appeared a table, set with a variety of dishes. Follin stared in amazement and Sorcha's face lit with joy.

"Oh, my, this is wondrous!" she exclaimed clapping her hands. "Sox, you are such a marvel," said Sorcha joining the children as they hugged a delighted Sox.

At that moment Ziggy remembered the gifts from his cousin, Tataria, and produced the wooden balls and cloth doll.

"Oh, Da!" exclaimed Tamotar and Lily together, "real toys! Thank you so much!"

Suddenly Follin felt a tug, it was Mage Saoirse calling them back. He sent an image showing the mages returning with an even greater force. Things had become so precarious that the Wood Elf clan had gathered to create a magical portal for Ziggy and his family's escape. Pandjar and his band of archers were at the River of Cups preparing to cross over to help them.

Ziggy placed his head in his hands and leaned his elbows on the table sobbing. The time they spent fighting the Wildlanders had robbed them of the time needed to convince Sorcha to return home.

Follin felt lost and confused. 'What should I do?' he asked himself.

Sox came to their rescue. He gently nudged the laughing children towards the cave entrance in readiness to leave. Next, he grasped Sorcha's hand in his mouth and led her to where Ziggy was seated. He barked three times, the same as he had done earlier, but this time it was focused on his master, Follin.

At each bark, Follin felt something shift inside his body. Closing his eyes briefly he examined the sensation. He recognised that this was a different application of the Cups change point, it linked him to Ziggy and Sorcha, he knew that they were ready for change.

Follin could feel the Elven couple's love but beneath was the fear of isolation and the fracturing of their reunion. He quickly wove a tapestry of energy binding the confused and grieving couple. The moment that he felt his own change point touch their hearts and minds, he pushed - this act culminated at the exact moment Sox barked one final time.

The cave returned to its previous drab and depressing state. The look on Sorcha's face was of complete and utter misery.

"Oh, Ziggy!" she cried, "I've missed you so much, please, please take us home. I can't live like this any longer." She put her arms around her husband's neck and fell into his arms.

The two elves cried at the grief of their loss and the joy of finding each other, their bodies heaving and shuddering with each sob. Follin had successfully engaged their change point but time was against him to do any more. Follin turned to arrange for the children's departure to their home.

"You mean we can leave this horrible place?" shouted Tamotar leaping to his feet. He had a wooden ball in one hand while the other held a bundle of stick toys – he threw the sticks away from him.

"Can we go and play with our cousins now?" cried Lily clutching tightly at both dolls, new and old. She let her old doll, clothed in filthy rags, drop to the ground.

"Yes," answered Follin, "you're going to your home in the forest to be with your clan."

"Yay!" the two children cried in unison.

Follin felt a little embarrassed to break up the lover's embrace but his father's urgent signal pressed them to hurry.

"We have to go, now! Come on you two, the children are waiting," he called as he waited at the cave entrance with the excited children.

Ziggy held his wife lovingly in his arms, they were like newlyweds. Sox barked loudly and led the family out of the cave. Follin stalled, he couldn't find the portal, the mist had deepened since their arrival. There came a different toned bark from Sox and he saw a light illuminating the elf's portal only a short distance from the cave.

"Hurry! It's closing!" screamed Follin as he lifted the two children and pushed them one by one through the fading portal. Ziggy and Sorcha ran and followed their children through, but just as they disappeared the portal closed. Follin had been left behind.

The first of the Wildlander mages appeared out of the mist, behind him came hundreds of warriors. They were led by the furious Mage Armitar. Upon seeing his enemy, Armitar jabbed with his staff at the lone figure. With a mighty scream, the evil mage sent a bolt of lightning towards his nemesis.

It was at that moment that Sox came to his master's rescue. With three rapid barks, the portal reappeared, just wide enough for Follin to stumble through, then it snapped shut.

Follin found himself lying on the floor of Tataria's hut. He snapped his head around and gasped in alarm. "Sox? Where is Sox?" He cast his eyes around the room. "He didn't follow me through the portal!"

Mage Saoirse helped his son to sit on the bed. "Son, calm down and start your water breathing as you have been taught. Let us see what that fae dog of yours is up to."

Within moments they saw Sox running along a dirt track in the forests near Sorcha's cave. To their surprise, Sox was greeted by a pack of fellow fae dogs. They played together until Sox noticed that he was being watched by his master. He barked goodbye to his friends, created a portal of his own and leapt into Follin's lap.

"I think that Sox has been watching over Sorcha and the children ever since he learned of Ziggy's loss. He must have asked his fae friends to keep guard when he was busy with me," Follin said proudly.

"What an amazing dog you have there, son," affirmed his father.

~

When Follin and Mage Saoirse left to be with Eve, Ziggy remained with his family in the Wood Elf village. He needed to spend time with his family. The clan elders agreed that the

Wildlanders were not an immediate threat to the village but they may be a threat to travellers. They decided that Ziggy's brother, Pandjar, an experienced Elf Ranger like his brother, should accompany Follin and his father to the City of Life.

Each evening Follin entered his water breathing meditation to make contact with Eve. While with his wife he could also enjoy the loving contact with his two unborn children.

During one of his meditations, Follin was contacted by the King and Queen of Cups. They wanted to know more about his adventures in the Shadowlands and particularly about Mage Armitar. They explained that the mage was as crafty as he was evil, a well-known enemy of the Tarot Empire and the Elven people.

The King explained that Mage Armitar had violated the tapestry of elemental magic at his death which permitted him to remain suspended between the world of the living and the dead. This allowed him to continue his magical manipulations to gather like-minded mages around him. The Cups monarchs were impressed when he told them of Sox's fae dog pack that protected Ziggy's family until they were rescued. They were even more amazed that Follin could borrow Pan's powers to panic the Wildlanders. Eventually, the conversation turned to his lessons of the Cups Kingdom.

"We know that you have studied Cups magic, Follin, but how have you fared with the Cups change point?" asked the Queen.

"I've finally learned how to use it," Follin replied proudly. "I used it to help Ziggy and Sorcha escape."

"Hmm? Please, tell us more," invited the King.

"I've studied the change points in three of the four Tarot Kingdoms, but this was the first time that I've had to weave them all together. At first, I used the Pentacles change point to locate Ziggy and Sorcha's energy centres. Then I applied the Swords change point to clarify the exact nature of their situation. I waited for the right moment, just as the lady of the Two of Swords picture showed me. Finally, I connected to Ziggy and Sorcha's Cups change point which was bound to their conflicted emotions. I was helped by Sox, he barked and that enabled me to unite them. You see, Ziggy had to decide if he should rescue Sorcha thus condemning her and his children to a life of fear in the forests as prey for the Wildlander mages, or to leave her happy in her delusions."

Follin continued. "Sorcha was muddled in her own mind too. She wanted to believe that the cave was real, that the shadows reflected on its walls were real events of the outer world. But deep down she knew that she and her children were in real danger. Sorcha had hidden her family in fear but had to reconcile the terrible impact of her decision on her children. She needed help to reach her change point."

"That was well done," said the Queen. "But did you really use Cups magic or was it simple persuasion?"

"It was definitely the Cups change point. The Cups are highly emotional creatures, everything they do is driven by unconscious urges and instincts which makes them vulnerable in a crisis. Their change point is entirely emotional. It seems to me, Your Majesties, that the Cups Kingdom is founded on emotion, not logic. I thought that the lion in the Two of Cups picture meant that it was a balance between the two – logic and emotion. It isn't half and half, it is 99% emotion and only 1% logic."

"You have done well under the most difficult of circumstances." The King turned to his wife. "Darling, do you have anything to add before Follin returns to his bed in the forest?"

"Yes, I do. Follin, your children will soon be born into this world. They have already mastered the water breathing technique and we know what that means don't we?"

Follin smiled. "Yes, they will be sensitive and fragile like the Cups. But I think Eve and I can teach them a few survival tricks. If we need to bring them down to earth we'll send them to the Pentacles Kingdom to slave under Master Pew and Page Alice."

~

Follin, his father, the Mage of Saoirse, and his Wood Elf escort, Pandjar, entered the City of Life in their filthy, mud-spattered clothes. The Mage called over his horse's neck to his two companions as they reached Follin's cottage, "I just want a hot bath, a proper cooked meal and a soft bed." But when they announced their arrival they found that everyone was in a flap readying for the twin's birth.

"Follin, how nice of you to drop by," announced a harassed Kahmia as the three travellers dragged themselves and their saturated haversacks through the back door. "We didn't know if you would make it in time or not."

She hurriedly sent the three to the covered porch where she directed them to place their wet clothing and gear before turning to Follin. "Eve is already in her birthing room in the Water Castle. If you are quick you might make it in time." She looked at the floor in horror then pushed him back outside to scrape the mud from his boots. Throwing him a change of clothes she yelled, "Now go and get changed and be quick about it!"

To Mage Saoirse and the Wood Elf, Kahmia offered refreshments then sent for The Hierophant, he could look after the new arrivals for now.

When Follin had changed into clean clothing Kahmia called to him, "Into the sea with you, and hurry!"

Follin had no time to unpack his travelling gear and that put him into a mind-spin of his own. Fortunately, Jon arrived and came to his rescue.

"Follin, forget about your bow and sword, I'll look after them, you've got more important things to attend to." Jon took hold of Follin's gear and handed them to a chuckling Hierophant. The Page then pushed the completely muddled father-to-be towards the beach.

"Go!" Jon ordered.

Follin found himself in a daze, surrounded by a large gathering of excited Cups who had been waiting to escort him to the Water Castle beneath the waves. He closed his eyes and forced himself to enter a state of calm, then slowly entered the water.

When he arrived at the castle, he sensed Eve calling him. The two lovers embraced and mind-spoke for some minutes until Eve sensed that the twins were ready.

"Love, the children have been waiting for you. They're now ready to enter this world."

Fiana arrived first, she smiled with joy as she was handed to her father. Aidan arrived a few minutes later.

Follin held Fiana close gifting his daughter with the radiant aura of his love. When she was placed in Eve's arms, Fiana could only stare into her mother's eyes, mesmerised by her mother's beauty. Eventually, Fiana came out of her entrancement, shook her head from side to side and went in search of Eve's breast. She wriggled and squirmed until she settled down to feed.

Where Fiana was active and inquisitive, Aidan was serene and observant. He calmly gazed at his surroundings, taking it all in, much as a warrior would do before battle. He eventually stared up at his father and smiled as his sister had done. When he was ready, and not before, Aidan said in a clear voice inside Follin's mind.

"Da, we waited for you."

With great concentration, Aidan guided his hand to touch Follin's open palm with his forefinger. In Follin's hand appeared a miniature magician's wand. Wrapping his tiny hand around it, Aidan said in a cheeky voice, "Look, Da, I have one too, just like yours and GrandDa's."

Eve fell in love with her twins all over again as she held them in her arms. She was infatuated with everything about them as she watched them nurse at her breast. Follin gathered his wife and children into his arms to lie with them on a large seaweed couch. He didn't want to miss a single second of this precious moment.

The King and Queen of Cups, the Royal Merrow, attended by Sir Rohan and the Pages Jon and Kahmia, soon arrived to bless the twins, then quietly withdrew to allow the family to settle into their Water Castle suite.

With the ocean currents swaying his couch, the excitement of his children's birth, and the debilitating fatigue from his rushed trip home through the mud and rain, Follin was soon sound asleep.

"Just like a man," shrugged one of the midwives. "The mother does all the work and it's the father who needs to sleep it off."

~

Follin's Meditation - Ten of Cups

This final image showed a family standing near their home under a rainbow of cups. In his meditation, Follin found himself in the garden of a courtyard similar to the one he and Eve shared while in the Pentacles Kingdom. There was a familiar figure working at the outside bench. He recognised the magician immediately, it was Mage Hermes.

The cottage was surrounded by flowers and vines, it had an autumn feel, golden leaves covered the ground. With a mighty embrace Mage Hermes welcomed his apprentice to his home and beckoned Follin to meld into his body. As he did so he could smell the flowers surrounding the cottage and he felt the infinity symbol above his head and below his feet. It kindled a golden light to illuminate the Alpha and Omega points of Follin's aura, much like a silkworm's golden cocoon.

"Now you know how The Emperor's Magician begins his day," the Mage chuckled. "Right, let's visit someone special."

Follin separated from the Mage and the two flew upwards into the clouds towards a simple timber and mud-brick cottage. They landed at the feet of the happy family from the Ten of Cups.

"Why are we visiting these people?" asked Follin in surprise.

"Just watch," Mage Hermes said patiently.

The Mage held his wand in his right hand then dramatically slammed its crystal tip into the ground. A bright golden light exploded under the cottage shaking the ground around them a moment or two.

The Ten of Cups man laughed delightedly at the energy released by the Mage's wand. His wife and children smiled in *wonder as they stood looking around at the aura surrounding them. As one they turned to see their house glowing like the crystal on the tip of Mage Hermes' wand. The man looked at the Mage and extended his hand in friendship.*

"Thank you, sir," he said to the Mage. They shook hands and the man walked with a light step into the house with his wife and their two children.

Follin turned to his mentor, "What was that all about?"

Mage Hermes answered: "This is a good man. He and his wife have created a wonderful life together. They are feeling down at the moment because things are not as easy as they should be. I planted a special energy form under their house. This will give them a lift and a few extra smiles that they will no doubt share with others."

Mage Hermes looked at his apprentice with a twinkle in his eye. "Sometimes we must remember that there are ordinary people in the world who could use a little magic just as much as the Tarot Empire's Sanctuary does. This is our folly, a gift to our community, and it is never wasted."

The End

~

The story concludes in book 5:
'The Fool's Journey through the Tarot Wands'

Astrological Correspondences with the Tarot

Water - Cancer, Scorpio and Pisces – Tarot Cups

These three astrological signs filter the world through their feelings before they engage their rational mind. This is primarily related to emotions and relationships. Water signs provide humanity with visions of unity and the joys of nurturing.

One could say that the Water signs provide the vision while the Fire signs, inspired by this vision, set off on a quest to achieve it; the Earth signs provide the physical and organisational means for the quest's success; and the Air signs communicate the process and final outcomes.

Water is the element of emotion and so the qualities that engage love and romance abound with these signs. The Water signs are sensitive, sympathetic, emotional, dreamers, affectionate and intuitive. Negative Water signs are emotionally unstable, irrational, needy, addictive, depressed, lonely and emotionally reactive. They experience life at an emotional level often struggling to gain control over their feelings. Their greatest fears are betrayal, loneliness and abandonment.

Water seeks to bring communion between people. For instance, the union of lovers, siblings, families and organisations. They can be controlling as they attempt to ensure no one wanders from the union that they have created. Because Water signs can be overly sensitive to abandonment and betrayal, it threatens to make them controlling, needy and moody.

Cancer reacts to their environment by nurturing others at the family level - they control through emotional means in their desire to keep everyone together.

Scorpio shows us that emotional energy can be both constructive and destructive – they can be extremely moody, passionate, intense, vindictive and emotionally dominating.

Pisces shows the rest of humanity that love is tangible and easily used and abused – they sometimes struggle to prevent themselves from dissolving into the void of universal consciousness. They help us share in their spiritual and artistic visions and dreams that inspire passion – they can be overwhelmed by their sensitivity to the environment and often mirror, or vibrate, to the moods of those around them.

Water keywords: Intimacy, nurturing, love, affection, resilience, union, community, nursing, empathy, compassion, abandonment, jealousy, betrayal, loss, moody, sensitive, grief, sadness, melancholy, loneliness, contentedness, neediness, emotional blackmail, manipulation, demanding, controlling, dreamy, lazy, genuine concern, support, companionship, trust, intuition.

Keywords – Cups Meanings

Ace of Cups - initiating intimacy and nurturing.

2 Cups - union, the emotional change point, connections, boundaries, romantic attraction, friendship, marriage, sharing, supporting, nurturing, helping, stand united, partnership, the emotional change point.

3 Cups - celebration, friendship, community, harvest, joyfulness, exuberance, bounty, networks, high spirits, social interactions.

4 Cups - sadness, withdrawal, avoiding a situation, reflection, depression, exhausted, closed-off, self-absorption, introspection, seeking solitude, apathetic, lacks motivation, ignoring offers of help or support, meditation, contemplation, disengaged.

5 Cups - pain of loss, new bridges to cross, sorrow, regret, denial, abandonment, betrayal, hopelessness, helplessness, grief, pain, lost opportunities, poor choices, a setback, suffering, endings, a final indulgence in grief before starting anew, lessons learned, beyond pain is opportunity, new growth, new adventures.

6 Cups - family, security and safety, nostalgia, social gatherings, unity, companionship, happiness, childhood, comfort, freedom, love, baby, home, sameness, goodwill, charity, giving, generosity, gifts, blessings, youth.

7 Cups – illusion, dreams, potential, choice, temptation, fantasy, wishful thinking, magic, visions, imagination, limitless possibilities, options, urges and desires, indulging in fantasy, escapism, dream on.

8 Cups - tying off loose ends, embarking on a new adventure, unfinished business, time to move on, new opportunities beckon, a journey, escaping, seeking greener pastures.

9 Cups - satisfaction, mentoring, life experience, good choices, earned wisdom, indulgent, contented, pleased, success, pleasure, abundance, confidence, competence, professional.

10 Cups - success, happy family, community, contentment, unity, communion, enjoyment, bliss, satisfaction, life is good, peace and harmony, well being, blessed, bonding, supportive social network, supportive extended family.

Page Cups - youthful sentimentality, rash exuberance, emotional, intuitive, intimate, caring, compassionate.

Knight Cups – enthusiasm, emotional, sensitive, refined, compassionate, a growing emotional maturity and intelligence.

Queen Cups - exhibits a mature balance in expressing emotions and compassion, master of the feminine Cups qualities.

King Cups - expresses tolerance and wisdom in the face of passion and empathy, master of the masculine Cups qualities.

Taoist Water Meditation

Believe it or not but there really is something known as a 'water meditation'. I have practised and studied Taoism, tai chi, chi kung and its many forms of meditation since 1980 under my teacher, Simon Lim. Simon was one of three students of Chen Tsu Tsu, one of the few surviving members of the Chen family, China. The Chen style is a water style which was used primarily for healing. As Simon taught in his backyard or in the local church hall, he would often say, "*soft, slow, continuous*". These words aptly sum up the Taoist water style of tai chi. Interestingly, Taoist water meditation is also known as Taoist Alchemy.

When I discovered tai chi I was absolutely smitten and practised all aspects of tai chi and Taoist meditation until it became a way of life. I was fortunate to have begun to feel, harness and move chi very early in my training. Within 6 months I was having out-of-body experiences and waking inside my dreams. I really was a keen student of the Tao. Here is a photo of myself and two of my children doing tai chi in the backyard (1987).

Everything we did as students of tai chi involved soft, slow movements, breathing in through the navel centre (dan tien), out through our hands and feeling suspended by a string while planting our feet deep into the earth. You will see Taoist practises in many of Follin and Eve's meditations and exercises throughout the Fool's Journey series.

Let me describe how I do the water meditation rather than stand back and try to explain it in third person. I always meditate in my recliner chair in the lounge room or lying on my bed. I don't meditate sitting in the lotus or other posture. I find that by lying down I can go so deep into trance that I am just a blob of jelly, no muscles, no bones and eventually I have no body.

I start each meditation with slow breathing to centre my breath at my navel chakra. Sometimes, if I am finding it hard to wind down, I will do a progressive relaxation to settle my physical body which automatically settles my mind. You will find these free meditations at www.soundcloud.com/noel-eastwood

You will have noticed that I sometimes have Follin fall asleep in his bathtub. When I was a child I would play in the bathtub and, holding my breath, I would slide underwater and stay there for as long as I could. If you have done this too, you will know that it is a strange yet pleasurable experience. The noises from outside and inside the bathtub sounded different, and the sensation of water surrounding my entire body made me feel safe and secure. These experiences were like falling asleep underwater, a metaphor for our mother's womb from whence we came into this world of matter.

Many years ago I had a dream that I was swimming underwater in Jervis Bay, not far from our home on the south coast of New South Wales, Australia. As a family, we spent many great times at the beach. In this dream I found myself swimming but to my surprise, I was also breathing. I wasn't breathing water or air, I was breathing chi, pure energy, under the water. I was so amazed that I woke up inside the dream. I was so charged with chi that I swam faster and faster, like a fish, like a shark on speed. My breath was centred at my navel centre, just as Follin and Eve are taught to do by their Archetype mentors. It was this experience that prompted me to include the water meditation in the Cups story.

    How do you practice the water meditation? I will run through it briefly here. The first stage in any meditation is always to relax. When I taught myself to meditate I would be happy to spend 19 minutes of a 20 minute meditation in relaxing every muscle in my body just to have that final minute of deep relaxation. My advice is for you to train yourself to first relax your body as deeply as possible.

    Secondly, it is through deep relaxation that you train yourself to access the passive water state. This means that you focus on letting go, go with the flow. Water flows and so too does your chi or life force. I start at the top and allow chi to flow downwards from my head and out through my hands and my feet. I would follow its flow with my mind. You can use the metaphor of warm honey flowing through your body. It enters through the top of your head and your shoulders then moves slowly into your chest and arms and abdomen. Feel it slowly fill you like warm honey as it flows down through the rest of your body and eventually out through the soles of your feet.

Remember that you are training your chi to flow passively like water, softly, slowly and continuously. Thus I use the words 'allow it to flow' rather than 'direct' or 'guide'.

I trained myself to follow this flow of chi all through my body until it exited through my fingers and toes. Even if it took most of the meditation to feel my chi I would stick with it. Sometimes I could only get it to flow down to my shoulders or elbows, if I couldn't feel my chi I would not stop until I could. With each breath, I would allow myself to go deeper and deeper into trance. The more I could turn to jelly the easier it was to feel the chi flowing through my body.

The essential element of Taoist meditation is to make it tactile, in other words, don't just 'see' it - 'feel' it. Start with imagining what it would feel like, then, with practice, you will actually feel your chi.

With dedicated practice, you will begin to experience lucid states and flashes of insight. You will fall asleep many times which actually helps you to enter these states. With practice, you will stay in the lucid state for longer and longer periods. With even more practice, you will achieve this lucid water state with only a few breaths. The secret is to learn the correct methods and not to give up.

What are the benefits of the water meditation? The Taoist water state allows you to tap into the fundamental 'nuts and bolts' of your psyche. It enhances your meditations guiding you towards greater spiritual growth, and it is one of the greatest aids in healing. Ultimately you will begin to dream. These dreams are special, they provide you with personal insight, inspire you to keep on doing your meditations, and they will guide your spiritual growth by showing you special ways to meditate and how to breathe chi through your body along specific pathways.

Performing regular water meditation helps you program your dreams before you go to sleep. The water state is basically your natural sleep state and once there you begin to heal as well as talk to ghosts, have out-of-body experiences and astral travel. You might want to read my self-hypnosis book to learn more about these exercises and read how others have used and benefited from them.

You may recall what the King of Cups said: "*The water breathing technique, which is necessary to undertake the Quest of Life, involves breathing the very essence that pervades the universe. This technique opens a doorway into dimensions beyond our own. The quest opens the practitioner to alternate planes of existence, however, very few practitioners are able to access even a small part of the spectrum that it makes available.*"

In this book, The Fool's Journey Through The Tarot Cups, I had Follin and Eve learn the water meditation for a very good reason: the Taoist water path really does lead to a deeper understanding of life and spirit. The best description I could think of in terms of its importance in Follin's story was to call it the 'Quest of Life'.

I look forward to introducing you to Follin and Eve's adventures in the Wands book where they are introduced to the phenomenal power of the Taoist fire meditation.

ABOUT THE AUTHOR

Noel Eastwood is a retired psychologist with over forty years professional experience in education, counselling and psychology. Now a full-time author, Noel shares his lifelong interests in depth Jungian psychotherapy, Taoist alchemy, meditation, tai chi, astrology and tarot. A gifted storyteller, his fiction and nonfiction works blend ancient wisdom and contemporary themes. His unique blend of hands-on experience and knowledge of these subjects, rollicking good storytelling and the wisdom of esoterica is evident in his books and audiobooks.

You can visit his website and subscribe to his free newsletters on the many diverse topics above - **www.plutoscave.com**

Other books by Noel Eastwood

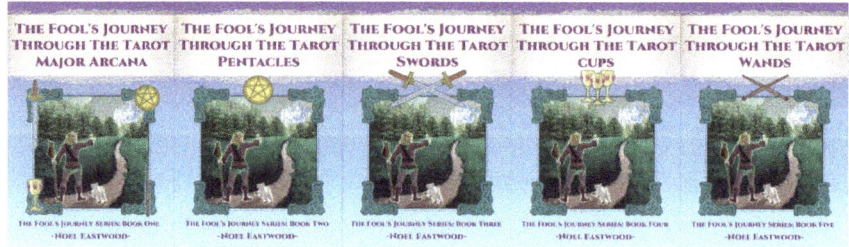

Get the series and the audiobooks narrated by Jonathan Johns.

www.ingramcontent.com/pod-product-compliance
Lightning Source LLC
Chambersburg PA
CBHW051537010526
44107CB00064B/2750